FRENCH WAYS AND THEIR MEANING

The republication of this work has been
made possible by a gift from

FONDS CHAMPAGNE
H E N R I O T
POUR L'ŒUVRE RETROUVÉE

FRENCH WAYS AND THEIR MEANING

BY

EDITH WHARTON

Introduction by Diane de Margerie

A Note and Suggestions for Further Reading
by Mary Ann Caws

EDITH WHARTON RESTORATION AT THE MOUNT
Lenox, Massachusetts

BERKSHIRE HOUSE PUBLISHERS
Lee, Massachusetts

Edition copyright © 1997 by Edith Wharton Restoration at The

ion may be
transmitted in any
ical, photocopying,
permission in
holder.

:ion Data

Wharton, Edith, 1862-1937.
   French ways and their meaning / by Edith Wharton :
introduction by Diane de Margerie : a note and suggestions for
further reading by Mary Ann Caws.
          p.   cm.
   Includes bibliographical references.
   ISBN 0-936399-87-2
   1. National characteristics, French.
   2. France—Civilization.
   3. French—Conduct of life. I. Margerie, Diane de. II. Caws, Mary
Ann. III. Title.
   DC34.W5 1997
   944—dc21
                                                         96-53346
                                                         CIP

ISBN 0-936399-87-2

Berkshire House books are available at substantial discounts for
bulk purchases by corporations and other organizations for
promotions and premiums. Special personalized editions can
also be produced in large quantities. For more information:

Berkshire House Publishers
480 Pleasant St., Suite 5
Lee, Massachusetts 01238

Printed in the United States of America
10 9 8 7 6 5 4 3 2 1

CONTENTS

AUTHOR'S NOTE (1919). — In the last two chapters of this book I have incorporated, in a modified form, the principal passages of two articles published by me respectively in *Scribner's Magazine* and in the *Ladies' Home Journal*, the former entitled "The French as seen by an American" (now called "In Conclusion"), the other "The New Frenchwoman."

PUBLISHERS' NOTE (1997). — The text of this book is a facsimile of the first edition published in 1919.

INTRODUCTION
By Diane de Margerie

If *French Ways and Their Meaning* enlightens us more on what Edith Wharton came to find in France than it does about the French, it may be due to the fact that within its pages she aligns her personal convictions to her conception of art, and expresses what she herself needed in order to live in a world of her own making.

This astute analysis of a people may, therefore, also be seen as an unintentional autobiography, one in which Wharton justifies her reasons for deciding to move to France. In it she informs us that everyone in France has "the seeing eye, the hearing ear." She — a lover of wit and anecdote who came from a family immersed in silence and secrecy, where words remained unspoken — must have found it both reassuring and appealing to partake in the free, ironic conversation at which the French are so adept.

The French woman seems perfect to her, and that thought is perhaps at the heart of the book. Wharton projected onto the French woman all the possibilities of which she herself felt capable: independence, courage, intellectual equality with men, and privileged masculine friendship. She, who admired George Sand and Madame de Sévigné, and who was — while living in France — the close friend of some of the greatest wits of the day, had suffered in silence for years among her own set in her own country.

The culminating idea of Edith Wharton's study of the French is that in France love merges with "the poetry of life," instead of being divided between body and soul as it is in a puritanical society. For a woman so conscious of separation, exile, and duality of being, nothing moved her more than the thought of this possible unity.

It is in this book that one gathers through Edith Wharton's visions and comments how much these pages are autobiographical; how — through her French experience — she was released to become herself. What she found in France was the freedom to utilize that which she already possessed: a profound insight that she was able to transmit into her novels, the majority of which she wrote while living here; and for that, we, the French, will always be grateful and proud.

Paris, October 1996

Translated by Judy Boullet

A NOTE AND SUGGESTIONS
FOR FURTHER READING
by Mary Ann Caws

> It takes a great deal of history to make
> a little tradition, a great deal of tradi-
> tion to make a little taste, and a great
> deal of taste to make a little art.
>
> Henry James[1]

In a letter from her Paris address at 53, rue
de Varenne of July 1919,[2] Wharton calls her
compilation of pieces about France, assembled
in wartime, "my disjointed little articles . . .
written, alas, not soberly and advisedly, as such
a theme demands, but in the brief and agitated
intervals between refugee committee meetings,
air-raids & bombardments. Be indulgent, therefore, & reconstruct out of the fragments the
little monument to the glory of France that my
scattered bricks were meant to build — if you
can!"[3] To the present-day reader, these scattered bricks may seem to have constructed a

remarkably cohesive, simple but telling commentary around the cluster of qualities she ascribes to the French, such as "taste, reverence, continuity, intellectual honesty" and also passion, and ascetic effort. If the French know how to live more slowly and more deeply than we do, if they are less likely to take risks and give of themselves, their long moral experience and sense of the fittingness of things enable them to savor what Wharton calls the poetry of life. The enviable manner in which they cherish and celebrate ideas with a passion unabated throughout wars and suffering guarantees their own endurance.

And what does America have to do with France and its intellectual glory in Wharton's eyes? It is, she claims, part of our own heritage, since Americans inherit "France through England and Rome and the Mediterranean culture, through France." As the conservative French people cling, however irritatingly, to each valley, each cave, and each custom throughout the ages, so we should celebrate, however different from ours it might be, the free and frank literature and culture of France with its own reflection of those customs. Around the world there is visible the "spilt glory" of what French ways and wisdom have left us, the traditions of the art and living France has always known to be inseparable.

What is astonishing is how little of this writing of an imported consciousness on the part of a "grateful alien," like her friend Henry James, seems outdated after all these years.[4] The very fact bears out Wharton's point about continuity. Perhaps indeed the blackberry still gives you fever, as the French peasant will tell you; in any case, her writing still stimulates. For we sense in this effulgent and yet balanced commentary about the French and the American ways of life the "incorrigible life-lover & life-wonderer" that Wharton termed herself. She has, like the French she understands so well, an ability to recognize, describe, and cherish "the marvel of things as they are." She loves the French spirit as it deserves to be loved, fearlessly. She speaks from the depths of an honorary and honorable French soul.

New York, October 1996

1. Henry James, quoted by Edith Wharton, in "The Man of Letters," in *The American Scene: the Quarterly Review*, July 1920, p. 198. The friends were equally passionate pilgrims, to use his phrase. See, for example, his *English Hours,* with an introduction by Leon Edel (New York and Oxford: Oxford University Press, 1981). Also his *Italian Hours* and Wharton's writings on Italy and the others on France.

2. She had moved to 53, rue de Varenne from an apartment at 58, rue de Varenne in 1910, and would move in 1919 to the Pavillon Colombe (a villa originally called Jean-Marie) in St.-Brice-sous-Forêt, where she stayed from July through November, and her chateau in Hyères in the Midi, called Sainte-Claire-du-Vieux-Château, where she stayed from December to June. After 1911, she was to live in France until her death in 1937.

3. In a letter to Barrett Wendell, from *The Letters of Edith Wharton,* ed. R.W.B. Lewis and Nancy Lewis (New York: Scribner's, 1988), p. 263. These articles were originally written for American soldiers and sailors, to help them understand the people and customs of France — the collection was in fact placed in all ship libraries, on the orders of the U.S. Department of the Navy. During the war, Wharton was heavily concerned in relief projects, among which were the American Hostels for Refugees and the Children of Flanders Rescue Committee. (Information from *Edith Wharton Abroad*, ed. Sarah Bird Wright, New York: St. Martin's Press, 1996, pp. 7-8 and 29-32.)

4. One reservation is so obvious as to need no commentary: I assume most of us, reading her now on both sides of the Atlantic, are likely to believe women can talk as well as they can listen, even in France. I may, of course, be wrong in my assumption.

SOME SELECTED FURTHER READING

WHARTON'S WRITINGS:

Wharton, Edith. *The Custom of the Country*. New York: Scribner's, 1913.

_____. *Madame de Treymes*. New York: Scribner's, 1907.

_____. *A Motor-flight Through France*. New York: Scribner's, 1908.

Wright, Sarah Bird, ed. *Edith Wharton Abroad: Selected Travel Writings, 1888-1920*. New York: St. Martin's Press, 1996.

ABOUT EDITH WHARTON:

Benstock, Shari. *No Gifts from Chance: A Biography of Edith Wharton*. New York: Scribner's, 1994.

Dwight, Eleanor. *Edith Wharton: An Extraordinary Life: An Illustrated Biography*. New York: Abrams, 1994.

Goodwyn, Janet. *Edith Wharton: Traveller in the Land of Letters*. London: Macmillan, 1990.

Joslin, Katherine, and Alan Price, eds. *Wretched Exotic: Essays on Edith Wharton in Europe*. New York: Peter Lang, 1993.

Lewis, R.W.B. *Edith Wharton: A Biography*. New York: Fromm International Publishing, 1975.

Price, Alan. *The End of the Age of Innocence: Edith Wharton and the First World War*. New York: St. Martin's Press, 1996.

Wolff, Cynthia Griffin. *A Feast of Words: The Triumph of Edith Wharton*. New York: Oxford University Press, 1977.

ABOUT FRANCE:

Letters from Paris to *The New Yorker*: Janet Flanner, Jane Kramer, Adam Gopnik.

PREFACE

This book is essentially a desultory book, the result of intermittent observation, and often, no doubt, of rash assumption. Having been written in Paris, at odd moments, during the last two years of the war, it could hardly be more than a series of disjointed notes; and the excuse for its publication lies in the fact that the very conditions which made more consecutive work impossible also gave unprecedented opportunities for quick notation.

The world since 1914 has been like a house on fire. All the lodgers are on the stairs, in dishabille. Their doors are swinging wide, and one gets glimpses of their furniture, revelations of their habits, and whiffs of their cooking, that a life-time of ordinary intercourse would not offer. Superficial differences vanish, and so (how much oftener) do superficial resemblances; while deep unsuspected similarities and disagreements, deep common attractions and repulsions, declare themselves. It is of these fundamental substances that the new link between France and America is made, and some reasons for the strength of the link ought to be discoverable in the suddenly bared depths of the French heart.

There are two ways of judging a foreign people: at first sight, impressionistically, in the manner of the passing traveller; or after residence among them, "soberly, advisedly," and with all the vain precautions enjoined in another grave contingency.

Of the two ways, the first is, even in ordinary times, often the most fruitful. The observer, if he has eyes and an imagination, will be struck first by the superficial dissemblances, and they will give his picture the sharp suggestiveness of a good caricature. If he settles down among the objects of his study he will gradually become blunted to these dissemblances, or, if he probes below the surface, he will find them sprung from the same stem as many different-seeming characteristics of his own people. A period of confusion must follow, in which he will waver between contradictions, and his sharp outlines will become blurred with what the painters call "repentances."

From this twilight it is hardly possible for any foreigner's judgment to emerge again into full illumination. Race-differences strike so deep that when one has triumphantly pulled up a specimen for examination one finds only the crown in one's hand, and the tough root still clenched in some crevice of prehistory. And as to race-resemblances, they are so often most misleading when they seem most instructive that any attempt to catch the likeness of another people by painting ourselves is never quite successful. Indeed, once the observer has gone beyond the happy stage when surface-differences have all their edge, his only chance of getting anywhere near the truth is to try to keep to the traveller's way, and still see his subject in the light of contrasts.

It is absurd for an Anglo-Saxon to say: "The Latin is this or that" unless he makes the mental reservation, "or at least seems so to me"; but if this mental reservation is always implied, if it serves always as the background of the picture, the features portrayed may escape caricature and yet bear some resemblance to the original.

Lastly, the use of the labels "Anglo-Saxon" and "Latin," for purposes of easy antithesis, must be defended and apologised for.

Such use of the two terms is open to the easy derision of the scholar. Yet they are too convenient as symbols to be abandoned, and are safe enough if, for instance, they are used simply as a loose way of drawing a line between the peoples who drink spirits and those who drink wine, between those whose social polity dates from the Forum, and those who still feel and legislate in terms of the primæval forest.

This use of the terms is the more justifiable because one may safely say that most things in a man's view of life depend on how many thousand years ago his land was deforested. And when, as befell our forbears, men whose blood is still full of murmurs of the Saxon Urwald and the forests of Britain are plunged afresh into the wilderness of a new continent, it is natural that in many respects they should be still farther removed from those whose habits and opinions are threaded through and through with Mediterranean culture and the civic discipline of Rome.

One can imagine the first Frenchman born into the world looking about him confidently, and saying: "Here I am; and now, how am I to make the most of it?"

The double sense of the fugacity of life, and of the many and durable things that may be put into it, is manifest in every motion of the French intelligence. Sooner than any other race the French have got rid of bogies, have "cleared the mind of shams," and gone up to the Medusa and the Sphinx with a cool eye and a penetrating question.

It is an immense advantage to have the primæval forest as far behind one as these clear-headed children of the Roman forum and the Greek amphitheatre; and even if they have lost something of the sensation "felt in the blood and felt along the heart" with which our obscurer past enriches us, it is assuredly more useful for them to note the deficiency than for us to criticise it.

The French are the most human of the human race, the most completely detached from the lingering spell of the ancient shadowy world in which trees and animals talked to each other, and began the education of the fumbling beast that was to deviate into Man. They have used their longer experience and their keener senses for the joy and enlightenment of the races still agrope for self-expression. The faults of France are the faults inherent in an old and excessively self-contained civilisation; her qualities are its qualities; and the most profitable way of trying to interpret French ways and their meaning is to see how this long inheritance may benefit a people which is still, intellectually and artistically, in search of itself.

HYÈRES, FEBRUARY, 1919.

FRENCH WAYS
AND THEIR
MEANING

I

FIRST IMPRESSIONS

I

HASTY generalisations are always tempting to travellers, and now and then they strike out vivid truths that the observer loses sight of after closer scrutiny. But nine times out of ten they hit wild.

Some years before the war, a French journalist produced a "thoughtful book" on the United States. Of course he laid great stress on our universal hustle for the dollar. To do that is to follow the line of least resistance in writing about America: you have only to copy what all the other travellers have said.

This particular author had the French gift of consecutive reasoning, and had been trained in the school of Taine, which requires the historian to illustrate each of his general conclusions by an impressive array of specific instances. Therefore, when he had laid down the principle that every American's ruling passion is money-making, he cast about for an instance, and found a striking one.

"So dominant," he suggested, "is this passion, that in cultivated and intellectual Boston —the Athens of America—which possesses a beautiful cemetery in its peaceful parklike suburbs, the millionaire money-makers, unwilling to abandon the quarter in which their most active hours have been spent, have created for themselves a burying-ground in the centre of the business district, on which they can look down from their lofty office windows till they are laid there to rest in the familiar noise and bustle that they love."

This literal example of the ruling passion strong in death seems to establish once for all the good old truth that the American cares only for money-making; and it was clever of the critic to find his instance in Boston instead of Pittsburg or Chicago. But unfortunately the cemetery for which the Boston millionaire is supposed to have abandoned the green glades of Mount Auburn is the old pre-revolutionary grave-yard of King's Chapel, in which no one has been buried since modern Boston began to exist, and about which a new business district has grown up as it has about similar carefully-guarded relics in all our expanding cities, and in many European ones as well.

It is probable that not a day passes in which the observant American new to France does not reach conclusions as tempting, but as wide of the mark. Even in peace times it was inevitable that such easy inferences should be drawn; and now that every branch of civilian life in France is more or less topsy-turvy, the temptation to generalise wrongly is one that no intelligent observer can resist.

It is indeed unfortunate that, at the very moment when it is most needful for France and America to understand each other (on small points, that is—we know they agree as to the big ones)—it is unfortunate that at this mo-

ment France should be, in so many superficial
ways, unlike the normal peace-time France,
and that those who are seeing her for the first
time in the hour of her trial and her great
glory are seeing her also in an hour of inevitable material weakness and disorganisation.

Even four years of victorious warfare
would dislocate the machinery of any great
nation's life; and four years of desperate resistance to a foe in possession of almost a tenth
of the national territory, and that tenth in-
dustrially the richest in the country, four such
years represent a strain so severe that one wonders to see the fields of France tilled, the mar-
kets provided, and life in general going on as
before.

The fact that France is able to resist such
a strain, and keep up such a measure of normal
activity, is one of the many reasons for admiring her; but it must not make newcomers forget that even this brave appearance of "business as usual" does not represent anything re-
sembling the peace-time France, with her

magnificent faculties applied to the whole varied business of living, instead of being centred on the job of holding the long line from the Yser to Switzerland.

In 1913 it would have been almost impossible to ask Americans to picture our situation if Germany had invaded the United States, and had held a tenth part of our most important territory for four years. In 1918 such a suggestion seems thinkable enough, and one may even venture to point out that an unmilitary nation like America, after four years under the invader, might perhaps present a less prosperous appearance than France. It is always a good thing to look at foreign affairs from the home angle; and in such a case we certainly should not want the allied peoples who might come to our aid to judge us by what they saw if Germany held our Atlantic sea-board, with all its great cities, together with, say, Pittsburg and Buffalo, and all our best manhood were in a fighting line centred along the Ohio River.

One of the cruellest things about a "people's war" is that it needs, and takes, the best men from every trade, even those remotest from fighting, because to do anything well brains are necessary, and a good poet and a good plumber may conceivably make better fighters than inferior representatives of arts less remote from war. Therefore, to judge France fairly to-day, the newcomer must perpetually remind himself that almost all that is best in France is in the trenches, and not in the hotels, cafés and "movie-shows" he is likely to frequent. I have no fear of what the American will think of the Frenchman after the two have fraternized at the front.

II

One hears a good deal in these days about "What America can teach France;" though it is worth noting that the phrase recurs less often now than it did a year ago.

In any case, it would seem more useful to leave the French to discover (as they are doing every day, with the frankest appreciation) what they can learn from us, while we Americans apply ourselves to finding out what they have to teach us. It is obvious that any two intelligent races are bound to have a lot to learn from each other; and there could hardly be a better opportunity for such an exchange of experience than now that a great cause has drawn the hearts of our countries together while a terrible emergency has broken down most of the surface barriers between us.

No doubt many American soldiers now in France felt this before they left home. When a man who leaves his job and his family at the first call to fight for an unknown people, because that people is defending the principle of liberty in which all the great democratic nations believe, he likes to think that the country he is fighting for comes up in every respect to the ideal he has formed of it. And perhaps some of our men were a little disappointed, and even discouraged, when they first came in contact with the people whose sublime spirit they had been admiring from a distance for three years. Some of them may even, in their first moment of reaction, have said to themselves: "Well, after all, the Germans we knew at home were easier people to get on with."

The answer is not far to seek. For one thing, the critics in question knew the Germans at home, *in our home,* where they had to talk our language or not get on, where they had to be what we wanted them to be—or get out. And, as we all know in America, no people on earth, when they settle in a new country, are more eager than the Germans to adopt its ways, and to be taken for native-born citizens.

The Germans in Germany are very different; though, even there, they were at great pains, before the war, not to let Americans find it out. The French have never taken the trouble to disguise their Frenchness from foreigners; but the Germans used to be very clever about dressing up their statues of Bis-

marck as "Liberty Enlightening the World"
when democratic visitors were expected. An
amusing instance of this kind of camouflage,
which was a regular function of their government, came within my own experience in 1913.

For the first time in many years I was in
Germany that summer, and on arriving in
Berlin I was much struck by the wonderful
look of municipal order and prosperity which
partly makes up for the horrors of its architecture and sculpture. But what struck me
still more was the extraordinary politeness of
all the people who are often rude in other
countries: post-office and railway officials, customs officers, policemen, telephone-girls, and
the other natural enemies of mankind. And I
was the more surprised because, in former
days, I had so often suffered from the senseless
bullying of the old-fashioned German em-
ployé, and because I had heard from Germans
that state paternalism had become greatly ag-
gravated, and that, wherever one went, petty

regulations were enforced by inexorable officials.

As it turned out, I found myself as free as air, and as obsequiously treated as royalty, and I might have gone home thinking that the German government was cruelly maligned by its subjects if I had not happened to go one evening to the Opera.

It was in summer, but there had been a cold rain-storm all day, and as the Opera House was excessively chilly, and it was not a full-dress occasion, but merely an out-of-season performance, with everybody wearing ordinary street clothes, I decided to keep on the light silk cloak I was wearing. But as I started for my seat I felt a tap on my shoulder, and one of the polite officials requested me to take off my cloak.

"Thank you: but I prefer to keep it on."

"You can't; it's forbidden. *Es ist verboten.*"

"Forbidden? Why, what do you mean?"

"His Majesty the Emperor forbids any lady

in the audience of the Royal and Imperial Opera House to keep on her cloak."

"But I've a cold, and the house is so chilly——"

The polite official had grown suddenly stern and bullying. "Take off your cloak," he ordered.

"I won't," I said.

We looked at each other hard for a minute —and I went in with my cloak on.

When I got back to the hotel, highly indignant, I met a German Princess, a Serene Highness, one of the greatest ladies in Germany, a cousin of his Imperial Majesty.

I told her what had happened, and waited for an echo of my indignation.

But none came. "Yes—I nearly always have an attack of neuralgia when I go to the Opera," she said resignedly.

"But do they make you take your cloak off?"

"Of course. It's the Emperor's order."

"Well—I kept mine on," I said.

Her Serene Highness looked at me incredulously. Then she thought it over and said: "Ah, well—you're an American, and American travellers bring us so much money that the Emperor's orders are never to bully them."

What had puzzled me, by the way, when I looked about the crowded Opera House, was that the Emperor should ever order the ladies of Berlin to take their cloaks off at the Opera; but that is an affair between them and their dressmaker. The interesting thing was that the German Princess did not in the least resent being bullied herself, or having neuralgia in consequence—but quite recognised that it was good business for her country not to bully Americans.

That little incident gave me a glimpse of what life in Germany must be like if you are a German; and also of the essential difference between the Germans and ourselves.

The difference is this: The German does not care to be free as long as he is well fed, well amused and making money. The Frenchman, like the American, wants to be free first of all, and free anyhow—free even when he might be better off, materially, if he lived under a benevolent autocracy. The Frenchman and the American want to have a voice in governing their country, and the German prefers to be governed by professionals, as long as they make him comfortable and give him what he wants.

From the purely practical point of view this is not a bad plan, but it breaks down as soon as a moral issue is involved. They say corporations have no souls; neither have governments that are not answerable to a free people for their actions.

III

This anecdote may have seemed to take us a long way from France and French ways; but it will help to show that, whereas the differences between ourselves and the French are mostly on the surface, and our feeling about the most important things is always the same, the Germans, who seem less strange to many of us because we have been used to them at home, differ from us totally in all of the important things.

Unfortunately surface differences—as the word implies—are the ones that strike the eye first. If beauty is only skin deep, so too are some of the greatest obstacles between peoples who were made to understand each other. French habits and manners have their roots in a civilisation so profoundly unlike ours— so much older, richer, more elaborate and firmly crystallised—that French customs necessarily differ from ours more than do those of more primitive races; and we must dig down to the deep faiths and principles from which every race draws its enduring life to find how like in fundamental things are the two people whose destinies have been so widely different.

To help the American fresh from his own land to overcome these initial difficulties, and to arrive at a quick comprehension of French character, is one of the greatest services that Americans familiar with France can render at this moment. The French cannot explain themselves fully to foreigners, because they take for granted so many things that are as unintelligible to us as, for instance, our eating corned-beef hash for breakfast, or liking mustard with mutton, is to them. It takes an outsider familiar with both races to explain away what may be called the corned-beef-hash differences, and bring out the underlying resemblances; and while actual contact in the trenches will in the long run do this more surely than any amount of writing, it may nevertheless be an advantage to the newcomer to arrive with a few first-aid hints in his knapsack.

The most interesting and profitable way of studying the characteristics of a different race is to pick out, among them, those in which our own national character is most lacking. It is sometimes agreeable, but seldom useful, to do the reverse; that is, to single out the weak points of the other race, and brag of our own advantages. This game, moreover, besides being unprofitable, is also sometimes dangerous. Before calling a certain trait a weakness, and our own opposite trait a superiority, we must be sure, as critics say, that we "know the context"; we must be sure that what appears a defect in the character of another race will not prove to be a strength when better understood.

Anyhow, it is safer as well as more interesting to choose the obviously admirable characteristics first, and especially those which happen to be more or less lacking in our own national make-up.

This is what I propose to attempt in these articles; and I have singled out, as typically "French" in the best sense of that many-sided term, the qualities of *taste, reverence, continuity,* and *intellectual honesty.* We are a new people, a pioneer people, a people destined by fate to break up new continents and experiment in new social conditions; and therefore it may be useful to see what part is played in the life of a nation by some of the very qualities we have had the least time to acquire.

II

REVERENCE

I

TAKE care! Don't eat blackberries! Don't you know they'll give you the fever?"

Any American soldier who stops to fill his cap with the plump blackberries loading the hedgerows of France is sure to receive this warning from a passing peasant.

Throughout the length and breadth of France, the most fruit-loving and fruit-cultivating of countries, the same queer conviction prevails, and year after year the great natural crop of blackberries, nowhere better and more abundant, is abandoned to birds and insects because in some remote and perhaps prehistoric past an ancient Gaul once decreed that "blackberries give the fever."

An hour away, across the Channel, fresh blackberries and blackberry-jam form one of the staples of a great ally's diet; but the French have not yet found out that millions of Englishmen have eaten blackberries for generations without having "the fever."

Even if they did find it out they would probably say: "The English are different. Blackberries have always given *us* the fever." Or the more enlightened might ascribe it to the climate: "The air may be different in England. Blackberries may not be unwholesome there, but here they are poison."

There is not the least foundation for the statement, and the few enterprising French people who have boldly risked catching "the fever" consume blackberries in France with as much enjoyment, and as little harm, as their English neighbours. But one could no more buy a blackberry in a French market than one could buy the fruit of the nightshade; the one is considered hardly less deleterious than the other.

The prejudice is all the queerer because the thrifty, food-loving French peasant has discovered the innocuousness of so many dangerous-looking funguses that frighten the Anglo-Saxon by their close resemblance to the poisonous members of the family. It takes a practised eye to distinguish cèpes and morilles from the deadly toadstool; whereas the blackberry resembles nothing in the world but its own luscious and innocent self. Yet the blackberry has been condemned untried because of some ancient taboo that the French peasant dares not disregard.

Taboos of this sort are as frequent in France as the blackberries in the hedges, and some of them interfere with the deepest instincts of the race.

Take, for instance, the question of dinner-giving. Dining is a solemn rite to the French, because it offers the double opportunity of good eating and good talk, the two forms of æsthetic enjoyment most generally appreciated. Everything connected with dinner-giving has an almost sacramental importance in France. The quality of the cooking comes first; but, once this is assured, the hostess' chief concern is that the quality of the talk shall match it. To attain this, the guests are as carefully chosen as boxers for a championship, their number is strictly limited, and care is taken not to invite two champions likely to talk each other down.

The French, being unable to live without good talk, are respectful of all the small observances that facilitate it. Interruption is considered the height of discourtesy; but so is any attempt, even on the part of the best talkers, to hold the floor and prevent others from making themselves heard. Share and share alike is the first rule of conversational politeness, and if a talker is allowed to absorb the general attention for more than a few minutes it is because his conversation is known to be so good that the other guests have been invited to listen to him. Even so, he must give them a chance now and then, and it is they who

must abstain from taking it, and must re-
peatedly let him see that for once they are
content to act as audience. Moreover, even
the privileged talker is not allowed to dwell
long on any one topic, however stimulating.
The old lady who said to her granddaughter:
"My dear, you will soon learn that an hour is
enough of anything" would have had to reduce her time-limit to five minutes if she had
been formulating the rules of French conversation.

In circles where interesting and entertain-
ing men are habitually present the women are
not expected to talk much. They are not, of
course, to sit stupidly silent, responsiveness
is their *rôle,* and they must know how to guide
the conversation by putting the right question
or making the right comment. But above all
they are not to air their views in the presence
of men worth listening to. The French care
passionately for ideas, but they do not expect
women to have them, and since they never
mistake erudition for intelligence (as we un-

educated Anglo-Saxons sometimes do) no woman can force her way into the talk by mere weight of book-learning. She has no place there unless her ideas, and her way of expressing them, put her on an equality with the men; and this seldom happens. Women (if they only knew it!) are generally far more intelligent listeners than talkers; and the rare quality of the Frenchwoman's listening contributes not a little to the flashing play of French talk.

Here, then, is an almost religious ritual, planned with the sole purpose of getting the best talk from the best talkers; but there are two malicious little taboos that delight in upsetting all these preparations.

One of them seems incredibly childish. It is a rule of French society that host and hostess shall sit exactly opposite each other. If the number at table is uneven, then, instead of the guests being equally spaced, they will be packed like sardines about one half the board, and left on the other with echoing straits between them thrown.

If the number is such that, normally seated, with men and women alternating, a lady should find herself opposite the hostess, that unthinkable sacrilege must also be avoided, and three women be placed together on one side of the table, and three men on the other. This means death to general conversation, for intelligent women will never talk together when they can talk to men, or even listen to them; so that the party, thus disarranged, resembles that depressing dish, a pudding in which all the plums have run into one corner.

The plums do not like it either. The scattered affinities grope for each other and vainly seek to reconstitute a normal pudding. The attempt is always a failure, and the French hostess knows it; yet many delightful dinners are wrecked on the unrelenting taboo that obliges host and hostess to sit exactly opposite each other.

"Precedence" is another obstacle to the real-

isation of the perfect dinner. Precedence in
a republic—! It is acknowledged to be an
absurd anomaly except where official rank is
concerned; and though its defenders argue
that it is a short-cut through many problems
of vanity and *amour-propre* it might certainly
be disregarded to the general advantage when-
ever a few intelligent people have been
brought together, not to compare their titles
but to forget them.

But there it is. The French believe themselves to be the most democratic people in the
world—and they have some of the democratic
instincts, though not as many as they think.
But an Academician must sit on his hostess'
right, unless there is a Duke or an Ambassa-
dor or a Bishop present; and these rules,
comic enough where peer meets prelate, become more humorous (and also grow more
strict) when applied to the imperceptible differences between the lower degrees of the immense professional and governmental hier-
archy.

But again—there it is. A hostess whose papa helped to blow up the Tuileries or pull down the Vendôme column weighs the relative claims of two Academicians (always a bad stumbling block) as carefully as a duchess of the old régime, brought up to believe in the divine right of Kings, scrutinises the genealogy of her guests before seating them. And this strict observance of rules is not due to snobbishness; the French are not a snobbish people. It is part of *les bienséances,* of the always-have-beens; and there is a big bullying taboo in the way of changing it.

In England, where precedence has, at any rate, the support of a court, where it is, so to speak, still a "going concern," and works automatically, the hostess, if she is a woman of the world, casts it to the winds on informal occasions; but in France there is no democratic dinner-table over which it does not permanently hang its pall.

II

It may seem curious to have chosen the instance of the blackberry as the text of a homily on "Reverence." Why not have substituted as a title "Prejudice"—or simply "Stupidity"?

Well—"Prejudice" and "Reverence," oftener than one thinks, are overlapping terms, and it seems fairer to choose the one of the two that is not what the French call "péjorative." As for "Stupidity"—it must be remembered that the French peasant thinks it incredibly stupid of us not instantly to distinguish a mushroom from a toadstool, or any of the intermediate forms of edible funguses from their death-dealing cousins! Remember that we Americans deprive ourselves of many delicious dishes, and occasionally hurry whole harmless families to the grave, through not taking the trouble to examine and compare the small number of mushrooms at our disposal; while the French avoid blackberries from a deep and awesome conviction handed down from the night of history.

There is the key to my apologue. The French fear of the blackberry is not due to any lack of curiosity about its qualities, but to respect for some ancient sanction which prevents those qualities from being investigated.

There is a reflex of negation, of rejection, at the very root of the French character: an instinctive recoil from the new, the untasted, the untested, like the retracting of an insect's feelers at contact with an unfamiliar object; and no one can hope to understand the French without bearing in mind that this unquestioning respect for rules of which the meaning is forgotten acts as a perpetual necessary check to the idol-breaking instinct of the freest minds in the world.

It may sound like a poor paradox to say that the French are traditional about small things because they are so free about big ones. But the history of human societies seems to show that if they are to endure they must unconsciously secrete the corrective of their own highest qualities.

"Reverence" may be the wasteful fear of an old taboo; but it is also the sense of the preciousness of long accumulations of experience. The quintessential is precious because whatever survives the close filtering of time is likely to answer to some deep racial need, moral or æsthetic. It is stupid to deprive one's self of blackberries for a reason one has forgotten; but what should we say of a people who had torn down their cathedrals when they ceased to feel the beauty of Gothic architecture, as the French had ceased to feel it in the seventeenth century?

The instinct to preserve that which has been slow and difficult in the making, that into which the long associations of the past are woven, is a more constant element of progress than the Huguenot's idol-breaking hammer.

Reverence and irreverence are both needed to help the world along, and each is most needed where the other most naturally abounds.

In this respect France and America are in the same case. America, because of her origin, tends to irreverence, impatience, to all sorts of rash and contemptuous short-cuts; France, for the same reason, to routine, precedent, tradition, the beaten path. Therefore it ought to help each nation to apply to herself the corrective of the other's example; and America can profit more by seeking to find out why France is reverent, and what she reveres, than by trying to inoculate her with a flippant disregard of her own past.

The first thing to do is to try to find out why a people, so free and active of thought as the French, are so subject to traditions that have lost their meaning.

The fundamental cause is probably geographical. We Americans have hitherto been geographically self-contained, and until this war did away with distances we were free to try any social and political experiments we pleased, without, at any rate, weakening ourselves in relation to our neighbours. To keep *them* off we did not even have to have an army!

France, on the contrary, has had to fight for her existence ever since she has had any. Of her, more than of any other great modern nation, it may be said that from the start she has had, as Goethe puts it, to "reconquer each day the liberty won the day before."

Again and again, in the past, she has seen her territory invaded, her monuments destroyed, her institutions shattered; the ground on which the future of the world is now being fought for is literally the same as that Catalaunian plain (the "Camp de Châlons") on which Attila tried to strangle France over fourteen hundred years ago. "In the year 450 all Gaul was filled with terror; for the dreaded Attila, with a host of strange figures, Huns, Tartars, Teutons, head of an empire of true barbarians, drew near her borders. Barbarism . . . now threatened the world. It had levied a shameful tribute on Constantinople; it now threatened the farthest West.

If Gaul fell, Spain would fall, and Italy, and Rome; and Attila would reign supreme, with an empire of desolation, over the whole world."*

"The whole world" is a bigger place nowadays, and "farthest West" is at the Golden Gate and not at the Pillars of Hercules; but otherwise might we not be reading a leader in yesterday's paper?

Try to picture life under such continual menace of death, and see how in an industrious, intelligent and beauty-loving race it must inevitably produce two strong passions:

Pious love of every yard of the soil and every stone of the houses.

Intense dread lest any internal innovations should weaken the social structure and open a door to the enemy.

There is nothing like a Revolution for making people conservative; that is one of the reasons why, for instance, our Constitution, the child of Revolution, is the most conservative

---

*Kitchin: "History of France," vol. I.

in history. But, in other respects, why should we Americans be conservative? To begin with, there is not much as yet for us to "conserve" except a few root-principles of conduct, social and political; and see how they spring up and dominate every other interest in each national crisis!

In France it is different. The French have nearly two thousand years of history and art and industry and social and political life to "conserve"; that is another of the reasons why their intense intellectual curiosity, their perpetual desire for the new thing, is counteracted by a clinging to rules and precedents that have often become meaningless.

III

Reverence is the life-belt of those whose home is on a raft, and Americans have not pored over the map of France for the last four years without discovering that she may fairly be called a raft. But geographical necessity is far from being the only justification of reverence. It is not chiefly because the new methods of warfare lay America open to the same menace as continental Europe that it is good for us to consider the meaning of this ancient principle of civilised societies.

We are growing up at last; and it is only in maturity that a man glances back along the past, and sees the use of the constraints that irritated his impatient youth. So with races and nations; and America has reached the very moment in her development when she may best understand what has kept older races and riper civilisations sound.

Reverence is one of these preserving elements, and it is worth while to study it in its action in French life. If geographical necessity is the fundamental cause, another, almost as deep-seated, is to be found in the instinct of every people to value and preserve what they have themselves created and made beautiful.

In Selden's "Table-talk" there is told the story of a certain carver of idols. Being a pious man he had always worshipped his own idols till he was suddenly called upon to make one in great haste, and, no other wood being available, had to cut down the plum-tree in his own garden and make the image out of that.

He could not worship the plum-tree idol, because he knew too much about the plum-tree. That, at least, is Selden's version; but how little insight it shows into human processes! Of course, after a time, the carver came to worship the plum-tree idol, and to worship it just because he had grown the tree and carved the image, and it was therefore doubly of his making. That is the very key to the secret of reverence; the tenderness we feel for our own effort extending to respect for all fine human effort.

America is already showing this instinct in her eagerness to beautify her towns, and to preserve her few pre-Revolutionary buildings —that small fragment of her mighty European heritage.

But there are whole stretches of this heritage that have been too long allowed to run to waste: our language, our literature, and many other things pertaining to the great undefinable domain of Taste.

A man who owns a vast field does not care for that field half as much when it is a waste as after he has sweated over its furrows and seen the seeds spring. And when he has turned a bit of it into a useless bright flower-garden he cares for that useless bit best of all.

The deeper civilisation of a country may to a great extent be measured by the care she gives to her flower-garden—the corner of her life where the supposedly "useless" arts and graces flourish. In the cultivating of that garden France has surpassed all modern nations; and one of the greatest of America's present opportunities is to find out why.

III

TASTE

I

FRENCH taste? Why, of course—everybody knows all about that! It's the way the women put on their hats, and the upholsterers drape their curtains.

Certainly—why not?

The artistic integrity of the French has led them to feel from the beginning that there is no difference in kind between the curve of a woman's hat-brim and the curve of a Rodin marble, or between the droop of an upholsterer's curtain and that of the branches along a great avenue laid out by Le Nôtre.

It was the Puritan races—every one of them non-creative in the plastic arts—who decided that "Art" (that is, plastic art) was something apart from life, as dangerous to it as

Plato thought Poets in a Republic, and to be
tolerated only when it was so lofty, unap-
proachable and remote from any appeal to
average humanity that it bored people to
death, and they locked it up in Museums to
get rid of it.

But this article is headed "Taste," and taste,
whatever it may be, is not, after all, the same
thing as art. No; it is not art—but it is the
atmosphere in which art lives, and outside of
which it cannot live. It is the regulating principle of all art, of the art of dress and of
manners, and of living in general, as well as
of sculpture or music. It is because the
French have always been so innately sure of
this, that, without burdening themselves with
formulas, they have instinctively applied to
living the same rules that they applied to artistic creation.

II

I remember being told when I was a young
girl: "If you want to interest the person you

are talking to, pitch your voice so that only that one person will hear you."

That small axiom, apart from its obvious application, contains nearly all there is to say about Taste.

That a thing should be in scale—should be proportioned to its purpose—is one of the first requirements of beauty, in whatever order. No shouting where an undertone will do; and no gigantic Statue of Liberty in butter for a World's Fair, when the little Wingless Victory, tying on her sandal on the Acropolis, holds the whole horizon in the curve of her slim arm.

The essence of taste is suitability. Divest the word of its prim and priggish implications, and see how it expresses the mysterious demand of eye and mind for symmetry, harmony and order.

Suitability—fitness—is, and always has been, the very foundation of French standards. Fitness is only a contraction of fittingness; and if any of our American soldiers in

France should pause to look up at the narrow niches in the portal of a French cathedral, or at the group of holy figures in the triangle or half-circle above, they are likely to be struck first of all by the way in which the attitude of each figure or group is adapted to the space it fills.

If the figure is cramped and uncomfortable —if the saint or angel seems to be in a strait-jacket or a padded cell—then the sculptor has failed, and taste is offended. It is essential that there should be perfect harmony between the natural attitude of the figure and the space it lives in—that a square saint should not be put in a round hole. Range through plastic art, from Chaldæa to France, and you will see how this principle of adaptation has always ruled composition.

III

It is the sense of its universal applicability that makes taste so living an influence in France. French people "have taste" as naturally as they breathe: it is not regarded as an accomplishment, like playing the flute.

The universal existence of taste, and of the standard it creates—it insists on—explains many of the things that strike Americans on first arriving in France.

It is the reason, for instance, why the French have beautiful stone quays along the great rivers on which their cities are built, and why noble monuments of architecture, and gardens and terraces, have been built along these quays. The French have always felt and reverenced the beauty of their rivers, and known the value, artistic and hygienic, of a beautiful and well-kept river-front in the heart of a crowded city.

When industrialism began its work of disfigurement in the great cities of the world, long reaches of the Thames were seized upon by the factory-builder, and London has only by a recent effort saved a short stretch of her river front; even so, from the Embankment, whether at Westminster or Chelsea, one looks across at ugliness, untidiness and squalor.

When industrialism came to the wise old Latin cities—Paris, Lyons, Bordeaux, Florence—their river banks were already firmly and beautifully built up, and the factory chimneys had to find a footing in the outskirts. Any American with eyes to see, who compares the architectural use to which Paris has put the Seine with the wasteful degradation of the unrivalled twin river-fronts of New York, may draw his own conclusions as to the sheer material advantage of taste in the creation of a great city.

Perhaps the most curious instance of taste-blindness in dealing with such an opportunity is to be found in Boston, where Beacon Street calmly turned its wealthy back to the bay, and fringed with clothes-lines the shores that might have made of Boston one of the most beautifully situated cities in the world. In this case, industry did not encroach or slums degrade. The Boston aristocracy appropriated the shore of the bay for its own residential uses, but apparently failed to notice that the bay was there.

Taste, also—the recognition of a standard —explains the existence of such really national institutions as the French Academy, and the French national theatre, the Théâtre Français. The history of the former, in particular, throws a light on much that is most distinctively French in the French character.

It would be difficult for any one walking along the Quai Malaquais, and not totally blind to architectural beauty, not to be charmed by the harmony of proportion and beauty of composition of a certain building with curved wings and a small central dome that looks across the Seine at the gardens of the Louvre and the spires of Saint Germain l'Auxerrois.

That building, all elegance, measure and balance, from its graceful cupola to the stately stone vases surmounting the lateral colonnades —that building is the old "Collège des Quatre

Nations," the Institute of France, and the home of the French Academy.

In 1635, at a time when France was still struggling with the heavy inheritance of feu-dalism, a bad man and great statesman, the mighty Cardinal Richelieu, paused in his long fight with the rebellious vassals of the crown to create a standard of French speech: "To establish the rules of the language, and make French not only elegant, but capable of deal-ing with the arts and sciences."

Think of the significance of such an act at such a moment! France was a welter of polit-ical and religious dissension; everything in the monarchy, and the monarchy itself, was in a state of instability. Austria and Spain menaced it from without, the great vassals tore it asunder from within. During the Great Assizes of Auvergne some of the most powerful of these nobles were tried, punished and stripped of their monstrous privileges; and the record of their misdeeds reads like a tale of Sicilian brigandage and Corsican vendetta.

Gradually the iron hand of Richelieu drew order—a grim pitiless order—out of this uninhabitable chaos. But it was in the very thick of the conflict that he seemed to feel the need of creating, then and there, some fixed principle of civilised life, some kind of ark in which thought and taste and "civility" could take shelter. It was as if, in the general upheaval, he wished to give stability to the things which humanise and unite society. And he chose "taste"—taste in speech, in culture, in manners,—as the fusing principle of his new Academy.

The traditional point of view of its founder has been faithfully observed for nearly three hundred years by the so-called "Forty Immortals," the Academicians who throne under the famous cupola. The Academy has never shrunk into a mere retreat for lettered pedantry: as M. Saillens says in his admirable little book, "Facts about France": "The great object of Richelieu was national unity," and "The Forty do not believe that they can keep the language under discipline by merely publishing a Dictionary now and then (the first edition came out in 1694). They believe that a standard must be set, and that it is for them to set it. Therefore the Academy does not simply call to its ranks famous or careful writers, but soldiers as well, bishops, scientists, men of the world, men of social rank, so as to maintain from generation to generation a national conservatory of good manners and good speech."

For this reason, though Frenchmen have always laughed at their Academy, they have always respected it, and aspired to the distinction of membership. Even the rebellious spirits who satirise it in their youth usually become, in maturity, almost too eager for its recognition; and, though the fact of being an Academician gives social importance, it would be absurd to pretend that such men as Pasteur, Henri Poincaré, Marshal Joffre,

sought the distinction for that reason, or that
France would have thought it worthy of their
seeking if the institution had not preserved
its original significance.

That significance was simply the safe-
guarding of what the French call *les choses
de l'esprit;* which cannot quite be translated
"things of the spirit," and yet means more
nearly that than anything else. And Richelieu and the original members of the Academy had recognised from the first day that
language was the chosen vessel in which the
finer life of a nation must be preserved.

It is not uncommon nowadays, especially in
America, to sneer at any deliberate attempts
to stabilise language. To test such criticisms it
is useful to reduce them to their last consequence—which is almost always absurdity. It
is not difficult to discover what becomes of a
language left to itself, without accepted
standards or restrictions; instances may be
found among any savage tribes without fixed
standards of speech. Their language speedily

ceases to be one, and deteriorates into a muddle of unstable dialects. Or, if an instance nearer home is needed, the lover of English need only note what that rich language has shrunk to on the lips, and in the literature, of the heterogeneous hundred millions of American citizens who, without uniformity of tradition or recognised guidance, are being suffered to work their many wills upon it.

But at this point it may be objected that, after all, England herself has never had an Academy, nor could ever conceivably have had one, and that whatever the English of America has become, the English of England is still the language of her great tradition, with perfectly defined standards of taste and propriety.

England is England, as France is France: the one feels the need of defining what the other finds it simpler to take for granted. England has never had a written Constitution; yet her constitutional government has long been the model of free nations. England's standards are all implicit. She does not feel the French need of formulating and tabulating. Her Academy is not built with hands, but it is just as powerful, and just as visible to those who have eyes to see; and the name of the English Academy is Usage.

IV

I said just now: "If any of our American soldiers look up at the niches in the portal of a French cathedral they are likely to be struck first of all by" such and such things.

In our new Army all the arts and professions are represented, and if the soldier in question happens to be a sculptor, an architect, or an art critic, he will certainly note what I have pointed out; but if he is not a trained observer, the chances are that he will not even look up.

The difference is that in France almost every one has the seeing eye, just as almost every one has the hearing ear. It is not a platitude, though it may be a truism, to say that the

French are a race of artists: it is the key that unlocks every door of their complex pyschology, and consequently the key that must be oftenest in the explorer's hand.

The gift of the seeing eye is, obviously, a first requisite where taste is to prevail. And the question is, how is the seeing eye to be obtained? What is the operation for taste-blindness? Or is there any; and are not some races—the artistically non-creative—born as irremediably blind as Kentucky cave-fishes?

The answer might be *yes,* in the case of the wholly non-creative races. But the men of English blood are creative artists too: theirs is the incomparable gift of poetic expression. And any race gifted with one form of artistic originality is always acutely appreciative of other cognate forms of expression. There has never been a race more capable than the English of appreciating the great plastic creators, Greece, Italy and France. This gift of the critical sense in those arts wherein the race does not excel in original expression seems an inevitable by-product of its own special endowment. In such races taste-blindness is purely accidental, and the operation that cures it is the long slow old-fashioned one of education. There is no other.

The artist races are naturally less dependent on education: to a certain degree their instinct takes the place of acquired discrimination. But they set a greater store on it than any other races because they appreciate more than the others all that, even to themselves, education reveals and develops.

It is just because the French are naturally endowed with taste that they attach such importance to cultivation, and that French standards of education are so infinitely higher and more severe than those existing in Anglo-Saxon countries. We are too much inclined to think that we have disposed of the matter when we say that, in our conception of life, education should be formative and not instructive. The point is, the French might return, what are we to be formed for? And, in any case, they would not recognise the antithesis, since they believe that, to form, one must instruct: instruct the eye, the ear, the brain, every one of those marvellous organs of sense so often left dormant by our Anglo-Saxon training.

It used to be thought that if savages appeared unimpressed by the wonders of occidental art or industry it was because their natural *hauteur* would not let them betray surprise to the intruder. That romantic illusion has been dispelled by modern investigation, and the traveller now knows that the savage is unimpressed because *he does not see* the new things presented to him. It takes the most complex assemblage of associations, visual and mental, to enable us to discover what a picture represents: the savage placed before such familiar examples of the graphic art as "The Infant Samuel" or "His Master's Voice" would not *see* the infant or the fox-terrier, much less guess what they were supposed to be doing.

As long as America believes in short-cuts to knowledge, in any possibility of buying taste in tabloids, she will never come into her real inheritance of English culture. A gentleman travelling in the Middle West met a charming girl who was a "college graduate." He asked her what line of study she had selected, and she replied that she had learnt music one year, and languages the next, and that last year she had "learnt art."

It is the pernicious habit of regarding the arts as something that can be bottled, pickled and absorbed in twelve months (thanks to "courses," summaries and abridgments) that prevents the development of a real artistic sensibility in our eager and richly endowed race. Patience, deliberateness, reverence: these are the fundamental elements of taste. The French have always cultivated them, and it is as much to them as to the eagle-flights of genius that France owes her long artistic supremacy.

From the Middle Ages to the Revolution

all the French trade-guilds had their travelling members, the "Compagnons du Tour de France." Not for greed of gold, but simply from the ambition to excel in their own craft, these "companions," their trade once learned, took their staves in hand, and wandered on foot over France, going from one to another of the cities where the best teachers of their special trades were to be found, and serving an apprenticeship in each till they learned enough to surpass their masters. The "tour de France" was France's old way of acquiring "Efficiency"; and even now she does not believe it can be found in newspaper nostrums.

IV

INTELLECTUAL HONESTY

I

MOST people, in their infancy, have made bogeys out of sofa-pillows and overcoats, and the imaginative child always comes to believe in the reality of the bogey he has manufactured, and toward twilight grows actually afraid of it.

When I was a little girl the name of Horace Greeley was potent in American politics, and some irreverent tradesman had manufactured a pink cardboard fan (on the "palmetto" model) which represented the countenance of the venerable demagogue, and was surrounded with a white silk fringe in imitation of his hoary hair and "chin-beard." A Horace Greeley fan had long been knocking about our country-house, and was a familiar object to me and to my little cousins, when

one day it occurred to us to make a bogey
with my father's overcoat, put Mr. Greeley's
head on top, and seat him on the verandah
near the front door.

When we were tired of playing we started
to go in; but there on the threshold in the
dusk sat Mr. Greeley, suddenly transformed
into an animate and unknown creature, and
dumb terror rooted us to the spot. Not one
of us had the courage to demolish that super-
natural and malevolent old man, or to dash
past him into the house—and oh, the relief it
was when a big brother came along and reduced him into his constituent parts!

Such inhibitions take the imagination far
back to the childhood of the human race,
when terrors and taboos lurked in every bush;
and wherever the fear of the thing it has
created survives in the mind of any society,
that society is still in its childhood. Intellectual honesty, the courage to look at things as
they are, is the first test of mental maturity.
Till a society ceases to be afraid of the truth in

the domain of ideas it is in leading-strings, morally and mentally.

The singular superiority of the French has always lain in their intellectual courage. Other races and nations have been equally distinguished for moral courage, but too often it has been placed at the service of ideas they were afraid to analyse. The French always want to find out first just what the conceptions they are fighting for are worth. They will not be downed by their own bogeys, much less by anybody else's. The young Oedipus of Ingres, calmly questioning the Sphinx, is the very symbol of the French intelligence; and it is because of her dauntless curiosity that France is of all countries the most *grown up*.

To persons unfamiliar with the real French character, this dauntless curiosity is supposed to apply itself chiefly to spying out and discussing acts and emotions which the Anglo-Saxon veils from publicity. The French view of what are euphemistically called "the facts of life" (as the Greeks called the Furies the

"Amiable Ones") is often spoken of as though it were inconsistent with those necessary elements of any ordered society that we call purity and morality. Because the French talk and write freely about subjects and situations that Anglo-Saxons, for the last hundred years (not before), have agreed not to mention, it is assumed that the French gloat over such subjects and situations. As a matter of fact, they simply take them for granted, as part of the great parti-coloured business of life, and no more gloat over them (in the morbid introspective sense) than they do over their morning coffee.

To be sure, they do "gloat" over their coffee in a sense unknown to consumers of liquid chicory and health-beverages: they "gloat," in fact, over everything that tastes good, looks beautiful, or appeals to any one of their acute and highly-trained five senses. But they do this with no sense of greediness or shame or immodesty, and consequently without morbidness or waste of time. They take the normal pleasures, physical and æsthetic, "in their stride," so to speak, as wholesome, nourishing, and necessary for the background of a laborious life of business or study, and not as subjects for nasty prying or morbid self-examination.

It is necessary for any one who would judge France fairly to get this fundamental difference fixed in his mind before forming an opinion of the illustrated "funny papers," of the fiction, the theatres, the whole trend of French humour, irony and sentiment. Well-meaning people waste much time in seeking to prove that Gallic and Anglo-Saxon minds take the same view of such matters, and that the *Vie Parisienne,* the "little theatres" and the light fiction of France do not represent the average French temperament, but are a vile attempt (by foreign agents) to cater to foreign pornography.

The French have always been a gay and free and Rabelaisian people. They attach a great deal of importance to love-making, but they consider it more simply and less solemnly than we. They are cool, resourceful and merry, crack jokes about the relations between the sexes, and are used to the frank discussion of what some one tactfully called "the operations of Nature." They are puzzled by our queer fear of our own bodies, and accustomed to relate openly and unapologetically the anecdotes that Anglo-Saxons snicker over privately and with apologies. They define pornography as a taste for the nasty, and not as an interest in the natural. But nothing would be more mistaken than to take this as proving that family feeling is less deep and tender in France than elsewhere, or the conception of the social virtues different. It means merely that the French are not frightened by the names of things; that they dislike what we call coarseness much less than what they call pruriency; and that they have too great a faith in the fundamental life-forces, and too much tenderness for the young mother suckling her baby, for Daphnis and Chloe in the orchard at dawn, and Philemon and Baucis on their threshold at sunset, not to wonder at our being ashamed of any of the processes of nature.

It is convenient to put the relations between the sexes first on the list of subjects about which the French and Anglo-Saxon races think and behave differently, because it is the difference which strikes the superficial observer first, and which has been most used in the attempt to prove the superior purity of Anglo-Saxon morals. But French outspokenness would not be interesting if it applied only to sex-questions, for savages are outspoken about those, too. The French attitude in that respect is interesting only as typical of the general intellectual fearlessness of France. She is not afraid of anything that concerns mankind, neither of pleasure and mirth nor of exultations and agonies.

The French are intrinsically a tough race: they are careless of pain, unafraid of risks, contemptuous of precautions. They have no idea that life can be evaded, and if it could be they would not try to evade it. They regard it as a gift so magnificent that they are ready to take the bad weather with the fine rather than miss a day of the golden year.

It is this innate intellectual honesty, the specific distinction of the race, which has made it the torch-bearer of the world. Bishop Butler's celebrated: "Things are as they are and will be as they will be" might have been the motto of the French intellect. It is an axiom that makes dull minds droop, but exalts the brain imaginative enough to be amazed before the marvel of things as they are.

II

Mr. Howells, I feel sure, will forgive me if I quote here a comment I once heard him make on theatrical taste in America. We had been talking of that strange exigency of the American public which compels the dramatist (if he wishes to be played) to wind up his play, whatever its point of departure, with the "happy-ever-after" of the fairy-tales; and I

had remarked that this did not imply a prefer-
ence for comedy, but that, on the contrary, our
audiences want to be harrowed (and even
slightly shocked) from eight till ten-thirty,
and then consoled and reassured before eleven.

"Yes," said Mr. Howells; "what the American public wants is *a tragedy with a happy
ending.*"

What Mr. Howells said of the American
theatre is true of the whole American attitude
toward life.

"A tragedy with a happy ending" is exactly
what the child wants before he goes to sleep:
the reassurance that "all's well with the
world" as he lies in his cosy nursery. It is a
good thing that the child should receive this
reassurance; but as long as he needs it he remains a child, and the world he lives in is a
nursery-world. Things are not always and
everywhere well with the world, and each man
has to find it out as he grows up. It is the
finding out that makes him grow, and until he

has faced the fact and digested the lesson he is not grown up—he is still in the nursery.

The same thing is true of countries and peoples. The "sheltered life," whether of the individual or of the nation, must either have a violent and tragic awakening—or never wake up at all. The keen French intelligence perceived this centuries ago, and has always preferred to be awake and alive, at whatever cost. The cost has been heavy, but the results have been worth it, for France leads the world intellectually just because she is the most grown up of the nations.

In each of the great nations there is a small minority which is at about the same level of intellectual culture; but it is not between these minorities (though even here the level is perhaps higher in France) that comparisons may profitably be made. A cross-section of average life must be taken, and compared with the same average in a country like ours, to understand why France leads in the world of ideas.

The theatre has an importance in France

which was matched only in the most glorious days of Greece. The dramatic sense of the French, their faculty of perceiving and enjoying the vivid contrasts and ironies of daily life, and their ability to express emotion where Anglo-Saxons can only choke with it, this innate dramatic gift, which is a part of their general artistic endowment, leads them to attach an importance to the theatre incomprehensible to our blunter races.

Americans new to France, and seeing it first in war-time, will be continually led to overlook the differences and see the resemblances between the two countries. They will notice, for instance, that the same kind of people who pack the music-halls and "movie-shows" at home also pack them in France. But if they will take a seat at the one of the French national theatres (the *Théâtre Français* or the *Odéon*) they will see people of the same level of education as those of the cinema-halls enjoying with keen discrimination a tragedy by Racine or a drama of Victor Hugo's. In

America the "movie" and music-hall audiences require no higher form of nourishment.
In France they do, and the Thursday mat-
inées in theatres which give the classic drama
are as packed as the house where "The Mys-
teries of New York" are unrolled, while on
the occasion of the free performances given
on national holidays in these theatres a line
composed of working-people, poor students
and all kinds of modest wage-earners forms
at the door hours before the performance be-
gins.

The people who assist at these great tragic
performances have a strong enough sense of
reality to understand the part that grief and
calamity play in life and in art: they feel
instinctively that no real art can be based on
a humbugging attitude toward life, and it is
their intellectual honesty which makes them
exact and enjoy its fearless representation.

It is also their higher average of education,
of "culture" it would be truer to say, if the
word, with us, had not come to stand for the

pretence rather than the reality. Education in its elementary sense is much more general in America than in France. There are more people who can read in the United States; but what do they read? The whole point, as far as any real standard goes, is there. If the ability to read carries the average man no higher than the gossip of his neighbours, if he asks nothing more nourishing out of books and the theatre than he gets in hanging about the store, the bar and the street-corner, then culture is bound to be dragged down to him instead of his being lifted up by culture.

III

The very significance—the note of ridicule and slight contempt—which attaches to the word "culture" in America, would be quite unintelligible to the French of any class. It is inconceivable to them that any one should consider it superfluous, and even slightly comic, to know a great deal, to know the best in every line, to know, in fact, as much as possible.

There are ignorant and vulgar-minded people in France, as in other countries; but instead of dragging the popular standard of culture down to their own level, and ridiculing knowledge as the affectation of a self-conscious clique, they are obliged to esteem it, to pretend to have it, and to try and talk its language—which is not a bad way of beginning to acquire it.

The odd Anglo-Saxon view that a love of beauty and an interest in ideas imply effeminacy is quite unintelligible to the French; as unintelligible as, for instance, the other notion that athletics make men manly.

The French would say that athletics make men muscular, that education makes them efficient, and that what makes them manly is their general view of life, or, in other words, the completeness of their intellectual honesty. And the conduct of Frenchmen during the last four and a half years looks as though there were something to be said in favour of this opinion.

The French are persuaded that the enjoyment of beauty and the exercise of the critical intelligence are two of the things best worth living for; and the notion that art and knowledge could ever, in a civilised state, be regarded as negligible, or subordinated to merely material interests, would never occur to them. It does not follow that everything they create is beautiful, or that their ideas are always valuable or interesting; what matters is the esteem in which *the whole race* holds ideas and their noble expression.

Theoretically, America holds art and ideas in esteem also; but she does not, as a people, seek or desire them. This indifference is partly due to awe: America has not lived long at her ease with beauty, like the old European races whose art reaches back through an unbroken inheritance of thousands of years of luxury and culture.

It would have been unreasonable to expect

a new country, plunged in the struggle with material necessities, to create an art of her own, or to have acquired familiarity enough with the great arts of the past to feel the need of them as promoters of enjoyment, or to understand their value as refining and civilising influences. But America is now ripe to take her share in the long inheritance of the races she descends from; and it is a pity that just at this time the inclination of the immense majority of Americans is setting away from all real education and real culture.

Intellectual honesty was never so little in respect in the United States as in the years before the war. Every sham and substitute for education and literature and art had steadily crowded out the real thing. "Get-rich-quick" is a much less dangerous device than "get-educated-quick," but the popularity of the first has led to the attempt to realise the second. It is possible to get rich quickly in a country full of money-earning chances; but there is no short-cut to education.

Perhaps it has been an advantage to the French to have had none of our chances of sudden enrichment. Perhaps the need of accumulating money slowly leads people to be content with less, and consequently gives them more leisure to care for other things. There could be no greater error—as all Americans know—than to think that America's ability to make money quickly has made her heedless of other values; but it has set the pace for the pursuit of those other values, a pursuit that leads to their being trampled underfoot in the general rush for them.

The French, at any rate, living more slowly, have learned the advantage of living more deeply. In science, in art, in technical and industrial training, they know the need of taking time, and the wastefulness of superficiality. French university education is a long and stern process, but it produces minds capable of more sustained effort and a larger range of thought than our quick doses of learning. And this strengthening discipline of the mind has preserved the passion for intellectual honesty. No race is so little addicted to fads, for fads are generally untested propositions. The French tendency is to test every new theory, religious, artistic or scientific, in the light of wide knowledge and experience, and to adopt it only if it stands this scrutiny. It is for this reason that France has so few religions, so few philosophies, and so few quick cures for mental or physical woes. And it is for this reason also that there are so few advertisements in French newspapers.

Nine-tenths of English and American advertising is based on the hope that some one has found a way of doing something, or curing some disease, or overcoming some infirmity, more quickly than by the accepted methods. The French are too incredulous of short-cuts and nostrums to turn to such promises with much hope. Their unshakeable intellectual honesty and their sound intellectual training lead them to distrust any way but the strait and narrow one when a difficulty is to be mastered or an art acquired. They are above all democratic in their steady conviction that there is no "royal road" to the worth-while things, and that every yard of the Way to Wisdom has to be travelled on foot, and not spun over in a joy-ride.

V

CONTINUITY

I

HAVE you ever watched the attempt of any one who does not know how to draw to put down on paper the roughest kind of representation of a house or a horse or a human being?

The difficulty and perplexity (to any one not born with the drawing instinct) caused by the effort of reproducing an object one can walk around are extraordinary and unexpected. The thing is there, facing the draughtsman, the familiar everyday thing—and a few strokes on paper ought to give at least a recognisable suggestion of it.

But what kind of strokes? And what curves or angles ought they to follow? Try and see for yourself, if you have never been taught to draw, and if no instinct tells you how. Evidently there is some trick about it which must be learned.

It takes a great deal of training and observation to learn the trick and represent recognisably the simplest three-dimensional thing, much less an animal or a human being in movement. And it takes a tradition too: it presupposes the existence of some one capable of handing on the trick, which has already been handed on to him.

Thirty thousand years ago—or perhaps more—there were men in France so advanced in observation and training of eye and hand that they could represent fishes swimming in a river, stags grazing or fighting, bison charging with lowered heads or lying down and licking their own shoulders—could even represent women dancing in a round, and long lines of reindeer in perspective, with horns gradually diminishing in size.

It is only twenty years ago that the first cavern decorated with prehistoric paintings

was discovered at Altamira, in north-western
Spain. Its discoverer was regarded with sus-
picion and contempt by the archæologists of
the period: they let him see that they thought
him an impostor and he died without having
been able to convince the learned world that
he had not had a hand in decorating the roof
of the cave of Altamira with its wonderful
troops of inter-glacial animals. But ten or
twelve years later the discovery of similar
painted caves in all directions north and south
of the Pyrenees at last vindicated Señor Sau-
tola's sincerity, and set the students of civilisation hastily revising their chronologies; and
since then proofs of the consummate skill of
these men of the dawn have been found on the
walls of caves and grottoes all over central and
southern France, throughout the very region
where our American soldiers have been camp-
ing, and where our convalescents are now
basking in the warm Mediterranean sun.

The study of prehistoric art is just beginning, but already it has been found that draw-

ing, painting and even sculpture of a highly developed kind were practised in France long before Babylon rose in its glory, or the foundations of the undermost Troy were laid. In fact, all that is known of the earliest historic civilisations is recent in date compared with the wonderful fore-shortened drawings and clay statues of the French Stone Age.

The traces of a very ancient culture discovered in the United States and in Central America prove the far-off existence of an artistic and civic development unknown to the races found by the first European explorers. But the origin and date of these vanished societies are as yet unguessed at, and even were it otherwise they would not count in our artistic and social inheritance, since the English and Dutch colonists found only a wilderness peopled by savages, who had kept no link of memory with those vanished societies. There had been a complete break of continuity.

II

In France it was otherwise.

Any one who really wants to understand France must bear in mind that French culture is the most homogeneous and uninterrupted culture the world has known. It is true that waves of invasion, just guessed at on the verge of the historic period, must have swept away the astounding race who adorned the caves of central and south-western France with drawings matching those of the Japanese in suppleness and audacity; for after that far-off flowering time the prehistorian comes on a period of retrogression when sculptor and draughtsman fumbled clumsily with their implements. The golden age of prehistory was over. Waves of cold, invasions of savage hordes, all the violent convulsions of a world in the making, swept over the earliest France and almost swept her away: almost, but not quite. Soon, Phœnicia and Greece were to reach her from the south, soon after that Rome was to stamp her once for all with the stamp of Roman citizenship; and in the intervals between these events the old, almost vanished culture doubtless lingered in the caves and river-beds, handed on something of its great tradition, kept alive, in the hidden nooks which cold and savages spared, little hearths of artistic vitality.

It would appear that all the while people went on obscurely modelling clay, carving horn and scratching drawings on the walls of just such river-cliff houses as the peasants of Burgundy live in to this day, thus nursing the faint embers of tradition that were to leap into beauty at the touch of Greece and Rome. And even if it seems fanciful to believe that the actual descendants of the cave-painters survived there can be little doubt that their art, or its memory, was transmitted. If even this link with the past seems too slight to be worth counting, the straight descent of French civilisation from the ancient Mediterranean culture which penetrated her by the Rhone and Spain and the Alps would explain the ripeness and the continuity of her social life. By her geographic position she seemed destined to centralise and cherish the scattered fires of these old societies.

What is true of plastic art must of course be true of the general culture it implies. The people of France went on living in France, surviving cataclysms, perpetuating traditions, handing down and down and down certain ways of ploughing and sowing and vine-dressing and dyeing and tanning and working and hoarding, in the same valleys and on the same river-banks as their immemorially remote predecessors.

Could anything be in greater contrast to the sudden uprooting of our American ancestors and their violent cutting off from all their past, when they set out to create a new state in a new hemisphere, in a new climate, and out of new materials?

How little the old peasant-tradition of rural England lingered among the uprooted colonists, who had to change so abruptly all their agricultural and domestic habits, is shown in the prompt disappearance from our impoverished American vocabulary of nearly all the old English words relating to fields and woods. What has become, in America, of the copse, the spinney, the hedgerow, the dale, the vale, the weald? We have reduced all timber to "woods," and, even that plural appearing excessive, one hears Americans who ought to know better speak of "*a* woods," as though the familiar word has lost part of its meaning to them.

This instance from our own past—to which might be added so many more illustrating the deplorable loss of shades of difference in our blunted speech—will help to show the contrast between a race that has had a long continuance and a race that has had a recent beginning.

The English and Dutch settlers of North America no doubt carried many things with them, such vital but imponderable things as prejudices, principles, laws and beliefs. But even these were strangely transformed when at length the colonists emerged again from the backwoods and the bloody Indian warfare. The stern experience of the pioneer, the necessity of rapid adaptation and of constantly improvised expedients, formed a far different preparation from that dogged resistance to invasion, that clinging to the same valley and the same river-cliff, that have made the French, literally as well as figuratively, the most conservative of western races. They also had passionate convictions and fierce wants, like other peoples trying to organise themselves; but the idea of leaving France in order to safeguard their convictions and satisfy their wants would never have occurred to the French Huguenots if the religious wars of the sixteenth century and the Revocation of the Edict of Nantes had not made France literally uninhabitable.   The English Puritans left England only to gain greater liberty for the independent development of their peculiar political and religious ideas; they were not

driven out with fire and sword as the Huguenots were driven from France.

Why, then, one wonders, did the French
people cling to France with such tenacity—
since none are more passionate in their convictions and prejudices where anything short
of emigration is concerned? They clung to
France because they loved it, and for such
sentimental fidelity some old underlying eco-
nomic reason usually exists. The map of
France, and the climate of France, show what
the reason was. France, as her historians
have long delighted to point out, is a country
singularly privileged in her formation, and
in the latitude she occupies. She is magnifi-
cently fed with great rivers, which flow where
it is useful for commerce and agriculture that
they should flow. The lines of her mountain-
ranges formed natural ramparts in the past,
and in the south and south-west, serve as great
wind-screens and sun-reflectors, creating almost tropic corners under a temperate latitude. Her indented coast opens into many ca-

pacious and sheltered harbours, and the course of the Gulf Stream bends in to soften the rainy climate of her great western peninsula, making Brittany almost as warm as the sunnier south.

Above all, the rich soil of France, so precious for wheat and corn-growing, is the best soil in the world for the vine; and a people can possess few more civilising assets than the ability to produce good wine at home. It is the best safeguard against alcoholism, the best incentive to temperance in the manly and grown-up sense of the word, which means voluntary sobriety and not legally enforced abstinence.

All these gifts France had and the French intelligently cherished. Between the Swiss snows and the icy winter fogs of Germany on the one side, and the mists and rain and perpetual dampness of England on the other, her cool mild sky shot with veiled sunlight overhung a land of temperate beauty and temperate wealth. Farther north, man might grow austere or gross, farther south idle and improvident: France offered the happy mean which the poets are forever celebrating, and the French were early aware that the poets were right.

III

Satisfaction with a happy mean implies the power to choose, the courage to renounce.

The French had chosen: they chose France. They had to renounce; and they renounced Adventure.

Staying in France was not likely to make any man inordinately rich in his life-time; forsaking France to acquire sudden wealth was unthinkable. The Frenchman did not desire inordinate wealth for himself, but he wanted, and was bound to have, material security for his children. Therefore the price to be paid for staying at home, and keeping one's children with one (an absolute necessity to the passionately tender French parent), was perpetual, sleepless, relentless thrift. The money necessary to security had to be accumulated slowly and painfully, so the Frenchman learned to be industrious, and to train his children to industry; and that money had to be kept fast hold of, since any profitable investment meant Risk.

Risk and Adventure were the two dreaded enemies that might, at a stroke, deprive one of the bliss of living in France, or of the modicum of well-being necessary to live there in comfort, as the unluxurious French understand it. Against Risk and Adventure, therefore, it is the French parent's duty to warn and protect his children. Brought up in this atmosphere of timidity and distrust of the unknown, generation after generation of young Frenchmen became saturated with the same fears; and those among them who tried to break through the strong network of tradition, and venture their inheritance or their lives in quest of new things, were restrained by the fierce conservatism of the women and the insinuating tyranny of French family life.

It is useless to deny that, to Anglo-Saxon eyes, the niggardliness of the French is their most incomprehensible trait. The reluctance to give, the general lack of spontaneous and impulsive generosity, even in times of such tragic appeal as the war has created, have too often astonished and pained those who most admire the French character to be passed over in any frank attempt to understand it.

During the most cataclysmic moments of the war, when it seemed that a few days or weeks might bring the world crashing down in ruins, and sweep away all that made life tolerable and material ease a thing worth considering—even then (though one could of course cite individual cases of the noblest generosity), the sense of the imprudence of uncalculated generosity still prevailed, and in France money never poured forth for the relief of suffering as it did in England.

The same clinging to tradition and fear of risk which make prudence almost a vice in the French are not applied only to money-saving. The French too often economise manners as they do francs. The discovery is disillusionising until one goes back to its cause, and learns to understand that, in a society based on caution, and built about an old and ineradicable bureaucracy, obsequiousness on the one side is sure to breed discourtesy on the other.

No one knows more than the French about good manners: manners are codified in France, and there is the possibility of an insult in the least deviation from established procedure, such as using the wrong turn in signing a note, as, for example, putting "Agréez, Monsieur" where "Veuillez agréer, Monsieur" is in order, or substituting "sentiments distingués" for "haute considération." Unfortunately, in the process, the forms of courtesy have turned into the sharp-edged metallic counters of a game, instead of being a spontaneous emission of human kindliness.

The French are kind in the sense of not being cruel, but they are not kindly, in the sense of diffused benevolence which the word implies to Anglo-Saxons. They are passionate and yet calculating, and simple uncalculated kindliness—the vague effusion of goodwill toward unknown fellow-beings—does not enter into a plan of life which is as settled, ruled off and barricaded as their carefully-measured and bounded acres. It savours too much of Adventure, and might lead one into the outer darknesses of Risk.

If one makes such a criticism to a French friend, in any candid discussion of race-differences, the answer is always: "Of course you Anglo-Saxons are more generous, because you are so much richer."

But this explanation, though doubtless sincere, is not exact. We are more generous not because we are richer, but because we are so much less afraid of being poor; and if we are less afraid of being poor it is due to the fact that our ancestors found it much easier to make money, not only because they were more

willing to take risks, but because more opportunities came in their way.

Once these arguments are balanced, it becomes easier to allow for French caution, and
to overlook it in favour of those other qualities which their way of life has enabled the
French to develop.

IV

First among these qualities is the power of
sustained effort, and the sense of its need in
any worth-while achievement.

The French, it has already been pointed
out, have no faith in short-cuts, nostrums or
dodges of any sort to get around a difficulty.
This makes them appear backward in the
practical administration of their affairs; but
they make no claim to teach the world practical efficiency. What they have to teach is
something infinitely higher, more valuable,
more civilising: that in the world of ideas, as
in the world of art, steady and disinterested
effort alone can accomplish great things.

It may seem, from what has been said in an earlier part of this chapter, as though the French were of all people the most interested, since questions of money so constantly preoccupy them. But their thoughts are not occupied with money-making in itself, as an end worth living for, but only with the idea of having money enough to be sure of not losing their situation in life, for themselves or their children; since, little as they care to rise in the world, they have an unspeakable terror of falling, based partly, no doubt, on the pitiful fate, in France, of those who *do* fall. This point assured, they want only enough leisure and freedom from material anxiety to enjoy what life and the arts of life offer. This absence of financial ambition should never be lost sight of: it is not only the best clue to the French character, but the most useful lesson our own people can learn from contact with France.

The requirements of the average Frenchman in any class are surprisingly few, and the ambition to "better" himself socially plays a very small part in his plans. What he wants is leisure to enjoy the fleeting good things of life, from which no one knows better how to extract a temperate delight, and full liberty of mind to discuss general ideas while pursuing whatever trade or art he is engaged in. It may seem an exaggeration to ascribe such aspirations to the average man of any race; but compared with other peoples the distinguishing mark of the Frenchman of all classes is the determination to defend his own leisure, the taste for the free play of ideas, and the power to express and exchange views on questions of general interest.

Great shrewdness and maturity of judgment result from this tendency to formulate ideas: it is unusual to hear a French peasant or working man express an opinion on life that is not sagacious. Human nature is a subject of absorbing interest to the French, and they have, to use their own phrase, "made the tour of it," and amply allowed for it in all their appreciations of life. The artless astonishment of the northern races in the face of the oldest of human phenomena is quite incomprehensible to them.

This serenity and maturity of view is the result of an immensely old inheritance of culture; and the first lesson it teaches is that Rome was not built in a day.

Only children think that one can make a garden with flowers broken from the plant; only inexperience imagines that novelty is always synonymous with improvement. To go on behaving as if one believed these things, and to foster their belief in others, is to encourage the intellectual laziness which rapid material prosperity is too apt to develop. It is to imprison one's self in a perpetual immaturity. The French express, perhaps unconsciously, their sense of the weight of their own long moral experience by their universal comment on the American fellows-in-arms whose fine qualities they so fully recognise. *"Ce sont des enfants*—they are mere children!" is what they always say of the young Americans: say it tenderly, almost anxiously, like people passionately attached to youth and to the young, but also with a little surprise at the narrow surface of perception which most of these young minds offer to the varied spectacle of the universe.

A new race, working out its own destiny in new conditions, cannot hope for the moral and intellectual maturity of a race seated at the cross-roads of the old civilisations. But America has, in part at least, a claim on the great general inheritance of Western culture. She inherits France through England, and Rome and the Mediterranean culture, through France. These are indirect and remote sources of enrichment; but she has directly, in her possession and in her keeping, the magnificent, the matchless inheritance of English speech and English letters.

Had she had a more mature sense of the value of tradition and the strength of continuity she would have kept a more reverent hold upon this treasure, and the culture won from it would have been an hundredfold greater. She would have preserved the language instead of debasing and impoverishing it; she would have learned the historic meaning of its words instead of wasting her time inventing short-cuts in spelling them; she would jealously have upheld the standards of its literature instead of lowering them to meet an increased "circulation."

In all this, France has a lesson to teach and a warning to give. It was our English forbears who taught us to flout tradition and break away from their own great inheritance; France may teach us that, side by side with the qualities of enterprise and innovation that English blood has put in us, we should cultivate the sense of continuity, that "sense of the past" which enriches the present and binds us up with the world's great stabilising traditions of art and poetry and knowledge.

VI

THE NEW FRENCHWOMAN

THERE is no new Frenchwoman; but the real Frenchwoman is new to America, and it may be of interest to American women to learn something of what she is really like.

In saying that the real Frenchwoman is new to America I do not intend to draw the old familiar contrast between the so-called "real Frenchwoman" and the Frenchwoman of fiction and the stage. Americans have been told a good many thousand times in the last four years that the real Frenchwoman is totally different from the person depicted under that name by French novelists and dramatists; but in truth every literature, in its main lines, reflects the chief characteristics of the people for whom, and about whom, it is written—

and none more so than French literature, the freest and frankest of all.

The statement that the real Frenchwoman is new to America simply means that America has never before taken the trouble to look at her and try to understand her. She has always been there, waiting to be understood, and a little tired, perhaps, of being either caricatured or idealised. It would be easy enough to palm her off as a "new" Frenchwoman because the war has caused her to live a new life and do unfamiliar jobs; but one need only look at the illustrated papers to see what she looks like as a tram-conductor, a taxi-driver or a munition-maker. It is certain, even now, that all these new experiences are going to modify her character, and to enlarge her view of life; but that is not the point with which these papers are concerned. The first thing for the American woman to do is to learn to know *the Frenchwoman* as she has always been; to try to find out what she is, and why she is what she is. After that it will be easy to see why the war has developed in her certain qualities rather than others, and what its after-effects on her are likely to be.

First of all, she is, in nearly all respects, as different as possible from the average American woman. That proposition is fairly evident, though not always easy to explain. Is it because she dresses better, or knows more about cooking, or is more "coquettish," or more "feminine," or more excitable, or more emotional, or more immoral? All these reasons have been often suggested, but none of them seems to furnish a complete answer. Millions of American women are, to the best of their ability (which is not small), coquettish, feminine, emotional, and all the rest of it; a good many dress as well as Frenchwomen; some even know a little about cooking— and the real reason is quite different, and not nearly as flattering to our national vanity. It is simply that, like the men of her race, the Frenchwoman is *grown up*.

Compared with the women of France the

average American woman is still in the kindergarten. The world she lives in is exactly like the most improved and advanced and scientifically equipped Montessori-method baby-school. At first sight it may seem preposterous to compare the American woman's independent and resonant activities—her "boards" and clubs and sororities, her public investigation of everything under the heavens from "the social evil" to baking-powder, and from "physical culture" to the newest esoteric religion—to compare such free and busy and seemingly influential lives with the artless exercises of an infant class. But what is the fundamental principle of the Montessori system? It is the development of the child's individuality, unrestricted by the traditional nursery discipline: a Montessori school is a baby world where, shut up together in the most improved hygienic surroundings, a number of infants noisily develop their individuality.

The reason why American women are not really "grown up" in comparison with the

women of the most highly civilised countries
—such as France—is that all their semblance
of freedom, activity and authority bears not
much more likeness to real living than the exercises of the Montessori infant. Real living,
in any but the most elementary sense of the
word, is a deep and complex and slowly-de-
veloped thing, the outcome of an old and rich
social experience. It cannot be "got up" like
gymnastics, or a proficiency in foreign languages; it has its roots in the fundamental
things, and above all in close and constant and
interesting and important relations between
men and women.

It is because American women are each other's only audience, and to a great extent each
other's only companions, that they seem, compared to women who play an intellectual and
social part in the lives of men, like children
in a baby-school. They are "developing their
individuality," but developing it in the void,
without the checks, the stimulus, and the discipline that comes of contact with the stronger

masculine individuality. And it is not only because the man is the stronger and the closer to reality that his influence is necessary to develop woman to real womanhood; it is because the two sexes complete each other mentally as well as physiologically that no modern civilisation has been really rich or deep, or stimulating to other civilisations, which has not been based on the recognised interaction of influences between men and women.

There are several ways in which the Frenchwoman's relations with men may be called more important than those of her American sister. In the first place, in the commercial class, the Frenchwoman is always her husband's business partner. The lives of the French bourgeois couple are based on the primary necessity of getting enough money to live on, and of giving their children educational and material advantages. In small businesses the woman is always her husband's bookkeeper or clerk, or both; above all, she is his business adviser. France, as you know, is held up to all other countries as a model of thrift, of wise and prudent saving and spending. No other country in the world has such immense financial vitality, such powers of recuperation from national calamity. After the Franco-Prussian war of 1870, when France, beaten to earth, her armies lost, half her territory occupied, and with all Europe holding aloof, and not a single ally to defend her interests—when France was called on by her conquerors to pay an indemnity of five thousand million francs in order to free her territory of the enemy, she raised the sum, and paid it off, *eighteen months sooner than the date agreed upon:* to the rage and disappointment of Germany, and the amazement and admiration of the rest of the world.

Every economist knows that if France was able to make that incredible effort it was because, all over the country, millions of French-women, labourers' wives, farmers' wives, small shopkeepers' wives, wives of big manufacturers and commission-merchants and bankers,

were to all intents and purposes their hus-
bands' business-partners, and had had a direct
interest in saving and investing the millions
and millions piled up to pay France's ransom
in her day of need. At every stage in French
history, in war, in politics, in literature, in art
and in religion, women have played a splen-
did and a decisive part; but none more splen-
did or more decisive than the obscure part
played by the millions of wives and mothers
whose thrift and prudence silently built up
her salvation in 1872.

When it is said that the Frenchwoman of
the middle class is her husband's business
partner the statement must not be taken in too
literal a sense. The French wife has less legal independence than the American or English wife, and is subject to a good many legal
disqualifications from which women have
freed themselves in other countries. That is
the technical situation; but what is the practical fact? That the Frenchwoman has gone
straight through these theoretical restrictions

to the heart of reality, and become her husband's associate, because, for her children's sake if not for her own, her heart is in his job, and because he has long since learned that the best business partner a man can have is one who has the same interests at stake as himself.

It is not only because she saves him a salesman's salary, or a book-keeper' salary, or both, that the French tradesman associates his wife with his business; it is because he has the sense to see that no hired assistant will have so keen a perception of his interests, that none will receive his customers so pleasantly, and that none will so patiently and willingly work over hours when it is necessary to do so. There is no drudgery in this kind of partnership, because it is voluntary, and because each partner is stimulated by exactly the same aspirations. And it is this practical, personal and daily participation in her husband's job that makes the Frenchwoman more grown up than others. She has a more interesting and more living life, and therefore she develops more quickly.

It may be objected that money-making is not the most interesting thing in life, and that the "higher ideals" seem to have little place in this conception of feminine efficiency. The answer to such a criticism is to be found by considering once more the difference between the French and the American views as to the main object of money-making—a point to which any study of the two races inevitably leads one back.

Americans are too prone to consider money-making as interesting in itself: they regard the fact that a man has made money as something intrinsically meritorious. But money-making is interesting only in proportion as its object is interesting. If a man piles up millions in order to pile them up, having already all he needs to live humanly and decently, his occupation is neither interesting in itself, nor conducive to any sort of real social development in the money-maker or in those about him. No life is more sterile than one into which nothing enters to balance such an output of energy. To see how different is the French view of the object of money-making one must put one's self in the place of the average French household. For the immense majority of the French it is a far more modest ambition, and consists simply in the effort to earn one's living and put by enough for sickness, old age, and a good start in life for the children.

This conception of "business" may seem a tame one to Americans; but its advantages are worth considering. In the first place, it has the immense superiority of leaving time for living, time for men and women both. The average French business man at the end of his life may not have made as much money as the American; but meanwhile he has had, every day, something the American has not had: Time. Time, in the middle of the day, to sit down to an excellent luncheon, to eat it quietly with his family, and to read his paper after-

ward; time to go off on Sundays and holidays
on long pleasant country rambles; time, almost any day, to feel fresh and free enough
for an evening at the theatre, after a dinner as
good and leisurely as his luncheon. And there
is one thing certain: the great mass of men and
women grow up and reach real maturity only
through their contact with the material reali-
ties of living, with business, with industry,
with all the great bread-winning activities;
but the growth and the maturing take place
in the intervals between these activities: and
in lives where there are no such intervals there
will be no real growth.

That is why the "slow" French business
methods so irritating to the American business man produce, in the long run, results
which he is often the first to marvel at and
admire. Every intelligent American who has
seen something of France and French life has
had a first moment of bewilderment on trying
to explain the seeming contradiction between
the slow, fumbling, timid French business

methods and the rounded completeness of French civilisation. How is it that a country which seems to have almost everything to learn in the way of "up-to-date" business has almost everything to teach, not only in the way of art and literature, and all the graces of life, but also in the way of municipal order, state administration, agriculture, forestry, engineering, and the whole harmonious running of the vast national machine? The answer is the last the American business man is likely to think of until he has had time to study France somewhat closely: it is that France is what she is because every Frenchman and every Frenchwoman takes time to live, and has an extraordinarily clear and sound sense of what constitutes *real living.*

We are too ready to estimate business successes by their individual results: a point of view revealed in our national awe of large fortunes. That is an immature and even childish way of estimating success. In terms of civilisation it is the total and ultimate result of a nation's business effort that matters, not the fact of Mr. Smith's being able to build a marble villa in place of his wooden cottage. If the collective life which results from our individual money-making is not richer, more interesting and more stimulating than that of countries where the individual effort is less intense, then it looks as if there were something wrong about our method.

This parenthesis may seem to have wandered rather far from the Frenchwoman who heads the chapter; but in reality she is at its very heart. For if Frenchmen care too much about other things to care as much as we do about making money, the chief reason is largely because their relations with women are more interesting. The Frenchwoman rules French life, and she rules it under a triple crown, as a business woman, as a mother, and above all as an artist. To explain the sense in which the last word is used it is necessary to go back to the contention that the greatness of France lies in her sense of the beauty and importance of living. As life is an art in France, so woman is an artist. She does not teach man, but she inspires him. As the Frenchwoman of the bread-winning class influences her husband, and inspires in him a respect for her judgment and her wishes, so the Frenchwoman of the rich and educated class is admired and held in regard for other qualities. But in this class of society her influence naturally extends much farther. The more civilised a society is, the wider is the range of each woman's influence over men, and of each man's influence over women. Intelligent and cultivated people of either sex will never limit themselves to communing with their own households. Men and women equally, when they have the range of interests that real cultivation gives, need the stimulus of different points of view, the refreshment of new ideas as well as of new faces. The long hypocrisy which Puritan England handed on to America concerning the danger of frank and free social relations between men and women has done more than anything else to retard real civilisation in America.

Real civilisation means an education that extends to the whole of life, in contradistinction to that of school or college: it means an education that forms speech, forms manners, forms taste, forms ideals, and above all forms judgment. This is the kind of civilisation of which France has always been the foremost model: it is because she possesses its secret that she has led the world so long not only in art and taste and elegance, but in ideas and in ideals. For it must never be forgotten that if the fashion of our note-paper and the cut of our dresses come from France, so do the conceptions of liberty and justice on which our republican institutions are based. No nation can have grown-up ideas till it has a ruling caste of grown-up men and women; and it is possible to have a ruling caste of grown-up men and women only in a civilisation where the power of each sex is balanced by that of the other.

It may seem strange to draw precisely this comparison between France, the country of all the old sex-conventions, and America, which is supposedly the country of the greatest sex-freedom; and the American reader may ask: "But where is there so much freedom of intercourse between men and women as in America?" The misconception arises from the confusion between two words, and two states of being that are fundamentally different. In America there is complete freedom of intercourse between boys and girls, but not between men and women; and there is a general notion that, in essentials, a girl and a woman are the same thing. It is true, in essentials, that a boy and a man are very much the same thing; but a girl and a woman—a married woman—are totally different beings. Marriage, union with a man, completes and transforms a woman's character, her point of view, her sense of the relative importance of things, far more thoroughly than a boy's nature is changed by the same experience. A girl is only a sketch; a married woman is the finished picture. And it is only the married woman who counts as a social factor.

Now it is precisely at the moment when her experience is rounded by marriage, motherhood, and the responsibilities, cares and interests of her own household, that the average American woman is, so to speak, "withdrawn from circulation." It is true that this does not apply to the small minority of wealthy and fashionable women who lead an artificial cosmopolitan life, and therefore represent no particular national tendency. It is not to them that the country looks for the development of its social civilisation, but to the average woman who is sufficiently free from bread-winning cares to act as an incentive to other women and as an influence upon men. In America this woman, in the immense majority of cases, has roamed through life in absolute freedom of communion with young men until the day when the rounding-out of her own experience by marriage puts her in a po-

sition to become a social influence; and from
that day she is cut off from men's society in all
but the most formal and intermittent ways.
On her wedding-day she ceases, in any open,
frank and recognised manner, to be an influence in the lives of the men of the community to which she belongs.

In France, the case is just the contrary.
France, hitherto, has kept young girls under
restrictions at which Americans have often
smiled, and which have certainly, in some respects, been a bar to their growth. The doing away of these restrictions will be one of
the few benefits of the war: the French young
girl, even in the most exclusive and most tra-
dition-loving society, will never again be the
prisoner she has been in the past. But this is
relatively unimportant, for the French have
always recognised that, as a social factor, a
woman does not count till she is married; and
in the well-to-do classes girls marry extremely
young, and the married woman has always had
extraordinary social freedom. The famous

French "Salon," the best school of talk and of ideas that the modern world has known, was based on the belief that the most stimulating conversation in the world is that between intelligent men and women who see each other often enough to be on terms of frank and easy friendship.   The great wave of intellectual and social liberation that preceded the French revolution and prepared the way, not for its horrors but for its benefits, originated in the drawing-rooms of French wives and mothers, who received every day the most thoughtful and the most brilliant men of the time, who shared their talk, and often directed it.   Think what an asset to the mental life of any country such a group of women forms!   And in France they were not then, and they are not now, limited to the small class of the wealthy and fashionable.   In France, as soon as a woman has a personality, social circumstances permit her to make it felt.   What does it matter if she had spent her girlhood in seclusion, provided she is free to emerge from it at the moment when she is fitted to become a real factor in social life?

It may, of course, be asked at this point, how the French freedom of intercourse between married men and women affects domestic life, and the happiness of a woman's husband and children. It is hard to say what kind of census could be devised to ascertain the relative percentage of happy marriages in the countries where different social systems prevail. Until such a census can be taken, it is, at any rate, rash to assert that the French system is less favourable to domestic happiness than the Anglo-Saxon. At any rate, it acts as a greater incentive to the husband, since it rests with him to keep his wife's admiration and affection by making himself so agreeable to her, and by taking so much trouble to appear at an advantage in the presence of her men friends, that no rival shall supplant him. It would not occur to any Frenchman of the cultivated class to object to his wife's friendship with other men, and the mere fact that he has the influence of other men to compete with is likely to conduce to considerate treatment of his wife, and courteous relations in the household.

It must also be remembered that a man who comes home to a wife who has been talking with intelligent men will probably find her companionship more stimulating than if she has spent all her time with other women. No matter how intelligent women are individually, they tend, collectively, to narrow down their interests, and take a feminine, or even a female, rather than a broadly human view of things. The woman whose mind is attuned to men's minds has a much larger view of the world, and attaches much less importance to trifles, because men, being usually brought by circumstances into closer contact with reality, insensibly communicate their breadth of view to women. A "man's woman" is never fussy and seldom spiteful, because she breathes too free an air, and is having too good a time.

If, then, being "grown up" consists in having a larger and more liberal experience of life, in being less concerned with trifles, and less afraid of strong feelings, passions and risks, then the French woman is distinctly more grown up than her American sister; and she is so because she plays a much larger and more interesting part in men's lives.

It may, of course, also be asked whether the fact of playing this part—which implies all the dangers implied by taking the open seas instead of staying in port—whether such a fact is conducive to the eventual welfare of woman and of society. Well—the answer to-day is: *France!* Look at her as she has stood before the world for the last four years and a half, uncomplaining, undiscouraged, undaunted, holding up the banner of liberty: liberty of speech, liberty of thought, liberty of conscience, all the liberties that we of the western world have been taught to revere as the only things worth living for—look at her, as the world has beheld her since August, 1914, fearless, tearless, indestructible, in face

of the most ruthless and formidable enemy the
world has ever known, determined to fight on
to the end for the principles she has always
lived for. Such she is to-day; such are the
millions of men who have spent their best
years in her trenches, and the millions of
brave, uncomplaining, self-denying mothers
and wives and sisters who sent them forth
smiling, who waited for them patiently and
courageously, or who are mourning them silently and unflinchingly, and not one of whom,
at the end of the most awful struggle in history, is ever heard to say that the cost has been
too great or the trial too bitter to be borne.

No one who has seen Frenchwomen since
the war can doubt that their great influence
on French life, French thought, French imagination and French sensibility, is one of the
strongest elements in the attitude that France
holds before the world to-day.

VII

IN CONCLUSION

I

ONE of the best ways of finding out why a race is what it is, is to pick out the words that preponderate in its speech and its literature, and then try to define the special meaning it gives them.

The French people are one of the most ascetic and the most laborious in Europe; yet the four words that preponderate in French speech and literature are: Glory, love, voluptuousness, and pleasure. Before the Puritan reflex causes the reader to fling aside the page polluted by this statement, it will be worth his while to translate these four words into *la gloire, l'amour, la volupté, le plaisir,* and then (if he knows French and the French well enough) consider what they mean in the language of Corneille and Pascal. For it must be understood that they have no equivalents in the English consciousness, and that, if it were sought to explain the fundamental difference between the exiles of the *Mayflower* and the conquerors of Valmy and Jéna, it would probably best be illustrated by the totally different significance of "love and glory" and "amour et gloire."

To begin with "la gloire": we must resign ourselves to the fact that we do not *really know* what the French mean when they say it—what, for instance, Montesquieu had in mind when he wrote of Sparta: "The only object of the Lacedæmonians was liberty, the only advantage it gave them was glory." At best, if we are intelligent and sympathetic enough to have entered a little way into the French psychology, we know that they mean something infinitely larger, deeper and subtler than we mean by "glory." The proof is that the Anglo-Saxon is taught *not* to do great deeds for "glory," while the French, unsurpassed in great deeds, have always avowedly done them for "la gloire."

It is obvious that the sense of duty has a large part in the French conception of glory: perhaps one might risk defining it as duty with a *panache*. But that only brings one to another untranslatable word. To put a *panache* —a plume, an ornament—on a prosaic deed is an act so eminently French that one seeks in vain for its English.equivalent; it would verge on the grotesque to define "la gloire" as duty wearing an aigrette! The whole conception of "la gloire" is linked with the profoundly French conviction that the lily *should* be gilded; that, however lofty and beautiful a man's act or his purpose, it gains by being performed with what the French (in a word which for them has no implication of effeminacy) call "elegance." Indeed, the higher, the more beautiful, the gesture or the act, the more it seems to them to call for adornment, the more it gains by being given relief. And thus, by the very appositeness of the word *relief,* one is led to perceive that "la gloire" as an incentive to high action is essentially the conception of a people in whom the plastic· sense has always prevailed. The idea of "dying in beauty" certainly originated with the Latin race, though a Scandinavian playwright was left, incongruously enough, to find a phrase for it.

The case is the same with "love" and "amour"; but here the difference is more visible, and the meaning of "amour" easier to arrive at. Again, as with "gloire," the content is greater than that of our "love." "Amour," to the French, means the undivided total of the complex sensations and emotions that a man and a woman may inspire in each other; whereas "love," since the days of the Elizabethans, has never, to Anglo-Saxons, been more than two halves of a word—one half all purity and poetry, the other all pruriency and prose. And gradually the latter half has been discarded, as too unworthy of association with the loftier meanings of the word, and "love" remains—at least in the press and in the household—a relation as innocuous, and as undisturbing to social conventions and business routine, as the tamest ties of consanguinity.

Is it not possible that the determination to keep these two halves apart has diminished the one and degraded the other, to the loss of human nature in the round? The Anglo-Saxon answer is, of course, that love is not license; but what meaning is left to "love" in a society where it is supposed to determine marriage, and yet to ignore the transiency of sexual attraction? At best, it seems to designate a boy-and-girl fancy not much more mature than a taste for dolls or marbles. In the light of that definition, has not license kept the better part?

It may be argued that human nature is everywhere fundamentally the same, and that, though one race lies about its deepest impulses, while another speaks the truth about them, the result in conduct is not very different. Is either of these affirmations exact? If human nature, at bottom, is everywhere the same, such deep layers of different habits, prejudices, and beliefs have been formed above its foundation that it is rather misleading to test resemblances by what one digs up at the roots. Secondary motives of conduct are widely divergent in different countries, and they are the motives that control civilised societies except when some catastrophe throws them back to the state of naked man.

To understand the difference between the Latin and the Anglo-Saxon idea of love one must first of all understand the difference between the Latin and Anglo-Saxon conceptions of marriage. In a society where marriage is supposed to be determined solely by reciprocal inclination, and to bind the contracting parties not only to a social but to a physical lifelong loyalty, love, which never has accepted, and never will accept, such bonds, immediately becomes a pariah and a sinner. This is the Anglo-Saxon point of view. How many critics of the French conception of love have taken the trouble to consider first their idea of marriage?

Marriage, in France, is regarded as founded for the family and not for the husband and wife. It is designed not to make two people individually happy for a longer or shorter time, but to secure their permanent well-being as associates in the foundation of a home and the procreation of a family. Such an arrangement must needs be based on what is most permanent in human states of feeling, and least dependent on the accidents of beauty, youth, and novelty. Community of tradition, of education, and, above all, of the parental feeling, are judged to be the sentiments most likely to form a lasting tie between the average man and woman; and the French marriage is built on parenthood, not on passion.

An illustration of the radical contradiction between such a view of marriage and that of the English races is found in the following extract from a notice of a play lately produced (with success) in London:

"After two months of marriage a young girl discovers that her husband married her because he wanted a son. *That is enough. She will have no more to do with him.* So he goes off to fulfil a mining engagement in Peru, and she hides herself in the country. . . ."

It would be impossible to exaggerate the bewilderment and disgust with which any wife or husband in France, whether young or middle-aged, would read the cryptic sentences I have italicised. "What," they would ask, "did the girl suppose he had married her for? And what did she *want* to be married for? And what is marriage for, if not for that?"

The French bride is no longer taken from a convent at sixteen to be flung into the arms of an unknown bridegroom. As emancipation has progressed, the young girl has been allowed a voice in choosing her husband; but what is the result? That in ninety-nine cases out of a hundred her choice is governed by the same considerations. The notion of marriage as a kind of superior business association, based on community of class, of political and religious opinion, and on a fair exchange of advantages (where one, for instance, brings money and the other position), is so ingrained in the French social organisation that the modern girl accepts it intelligently, just as her puppet grandmother bowed to it passively.

From this important act of life the notion of love is tacitly excluded; not because love is thought unimportant, but on account of its very importance, and of the fact that it is not conceivably to be fitted into any stable association between man and woman. It is because the French have refused to cut love in two that they have not attempted to subordinate it to the organisation of the family. They have left it out because there was no room for it, and also because it moves to a different rhythm, and keeps different seasons. It is because they refuse to regard it either as merely an exchange of ethereal vows or as a sensual gratification; because, on the contrary, they believe, with Coleridge, that

> "All thoughts, all passions, all delights,
>   Whatever stirs this mortal frame,
>   All are but ministers of Love,
>   And feed his sacred flame,"

that they frankly recognise its right to its own place in life.

What, then, is the place they give to the disturbing element? They treat it—the answer might be—as the poetry of life. For the French, simply because they are the most realistic people in the world, are also the most romantic. They have judged that the family and the state cannot be built up on poetry, but they have not felt that for that reason poetry was to be banished from their republic. They have decided that love is too grave a matter for boys and girls, and not grave enough to form the basis of marriage; but in the relations between grown people, apart from their permanent ties (and in the deepest consciousness of the French, marriage still remains indissoluble), they allow it, frankly and amply, the part it furtively and shabbily, but no less ubiquitously, plays in Puritan societies.

It is not intended here to weigh the relative advantages of this view of life and the other; what has been sought is to state fairly the reasons why marriage, being taken more seriously and less vaguely by the French, there remains an allotted place for love in their more precisely ordered social economy. Nevertheless, it is fairly obvious that, except in a world where the claims of the body social are very perfectly balanced against those of the body individual, to give such a place to passion is to risk being submerged by it. A society which puts love beyond the law, and then pays it such heavy toll, subjects itself to the most terrible of Camorras.

II

The French are one of the most ascetic races in the world; and that is perhaps the reason why the meaning they give to the word "volupté" is free from the vulgarity of our "voluptuousness." The latter suggests to most people a cross-legged sultan in a fat seraglio; "volupté" means the intangible charm that imagination extracts from things tangible. "Volupté" means the "Ode to the Nightingale" and the "Ode to a Grecian Urn;" it means Romeo and Juliet as well as Antony and Cleopatra. But if we have the thing, one may ask, what does the word matter? Every language is always losing word-values, even where the sense of the word survives.

The answer is that the French sense of "volupté" is found only exceptionally in the Anglo-Saxon imagination, whereas it is part of the imaginative make-up of the whole French race. One turns to Shakespeare or Keats to find it formulated in our speech; in France it underlies the whole view of life. And this brings one, of course, to the inevitable conclusion that the French are a race of creative artists, and that artistic creativeness requires first a free play of the mind on all the facts of life, and secondly the sensuous sensibility that sees beyond tangible beauty to the aura surrounding it.

The French possess the quality and have always claimed the privilege. And from their freedom of view combined with their sensuous sensibility they have extracted the sensation they call "le plaisir," which is something so much more definite and more evocative than what we mean when we speak of pleasure. "Le plaisir" stands for the frankly permitted, the freely taken, delight of the senses, the direct enjoyment of the fruit of the tree called golden. No suggestions of furtive vice degrade or coarsen it, because it has, like love, its open place in speech and practice. It has found its expression in English also, but only on the lips of genius: for instance, in the "bursting of joy's grape" in the "Ode to Melancholy" (it is always in Keats that one seeks such utterances) ; whereas to the French it is part of the general fearless and joyful contact with life. And that is why it has kept its finer meaning, instead of being debased by incomprehension.

III

The French are passionate and pleasure-loving; but they are above all ascetic and laborious. And it is only out of a union of these supposedly contradictory qualities that so fine a thing as the French temperament could have come.

The industry of the French is universally celebrated; but many—even among their own race—might ask what justifies the statement that they are ascetic. The fact is, the word, which in reality indicates merely a natural indifference to material well-being, has come, in modern speech, to have a narrower and a penitential meaning. It is supposed to imply a moral judgment, whereas it refers only to the attitude taken toward the creature comforts. A man, or a nation, may wear homespun and live on locusts, and yet be immoderately addicted to the lusts of the eye and of the flesh. Asceticism means the serene ability to get on without *comfort,* and comfort is an Anglo-Saxon invention which the Latins have never really understood or felt the want of. What they need (and there is no relation between the needs) is splendour on occasion, and beauty and fulness of experience always. They do not care for the raw material of sensation: food must be exquisitely cooked, emotion eloquently expressed, desire emotionally heightened, every experience must be transmuted into terms of beauty before it touches their imagination.

This fastidiousness, this tendency always to select and eliminate, and refine their sensations, is united to that stoic indifference to dirt, discomfort, bad air, damp, cold, and whatever Anglo-Saxons describe as "inconvenience" in the general organisation of life, from the bathroom to the banking system, which gives the French leisure of spirit for enjoyment, and strength of heart for war. It enables, and has always enabled, a people addicted to pleasure and unused to the discipline of sport, to turn at a moment's notice into the greatest fighters that history has known. All the French need to effect this transformation is a "great argument;" once the spring of imagination touched, the body obeys it with a dash and an endurance that no discipline, whether Spartan or Prussian, ever succeeded in outdoing.

This fearless and joyful people, so ardently individual and so frankly realistic, have another safeguard against excess in their almost Chinese reverence for the ritual of manners. It is fortunate that they have preserved, through every political revolution, this sense of the importance of ceremony, for they are without the compensating respect for the rights of others which eases intercourse in Anglo-Saxon countries. Any view of the French that considers them as possessing the instinct of liberty is misleading; what they have always understood is equality—a different matter—and even that, as one of the most acute among their recent political writers has said, "on condition that each man commands." Their past history, and above all the geographical situation which has conditioned it, must be kept in view to understand the French indifference to the rights of others, and the corrective for that indifference which their exquisite sense of sociability provides.

For over a thousand years France has had to maintain herself in the teeth of an aggressive Europe, and to do so she has required a strong central government and a sense of social discipline. Her great kings were forever strengthening her by their resistance to the scattered feudal opposition. Richelieu and Louis XIV finally broke this opposition, and left France united against Europe, but deprived of the sense of individual freedom, and needing to feel the pressure of an "administration" on her neck. Imagination, intellectual energy, and every form of artistic activity, found their outlet in social intercourse, and

France created polite society—one more work of art in the long list of her creations.

The French conception of society is hierarchical and administrative, as her government (under whatever name) has so long been. Every social situation has its appropriate gestures and its almost fixed vocabulary, and nothing, for example, is more puzzling to the French than the fact that the English, a race whose civilisation they regard as in some respects superior to their own, have only two or three ways of beginning and ending their letters.

This ritual view of politeness makes it difficult of application in undetermined cases, and therefore it often gets left out in emergencies. The complaint of Anglo-Saxons that, in travelling in France, they see little of the much-vaunted French courtesy, is not unjustified. The French are not courteous from any vague sense of good-will toward mankind; they regard politeness as a coin with which certain things are obtainable, and being no-

tably thrifty they are cautious about spending
it on strangers. But the disillusion of the
traveller often arises in part from his own ig-
norance of the most elementary French forms:
of the "Bon jour, Madame," on entering and
leaving a shop, of the fact that a visitor should
always, on taking leave, be conducted to the
outer door, and a gentleman (of the old
school) bidden not to remain uncovered when
he stops to speak to a lady in the street; of
the "Merci" that should follow every service,
however slight, the "Après vous" which makes
way, with ceremonious insistence, for the person who happens to be entering a door with
one. In these respects, Anglo-Saxons, by their
lack of "form" (and their lack of perception),
are perpetually giving unintentional offence.
But small social fashions are oddly different
in different countries and vary absurdly in suc-
ceeding generations. The French gentleman
does not uncover in a lift or in a museum, because he considers these places as public as the
street; he does not, after the manner of the

newest-of-all American, jump up like a Jack-in-the-box (and remain standing at attention) every time the woman he is calling on rises from her seat, because he considers such gymnastics fatal to social ease; but he is shocked by the way in which Americans loll and sprawl when they are seated, and equally bewildered by their excess of ceremony on some occasions, and their startling familiarity on others.

Such misunderstandings are inevitable between people of different speech and traditions. If French and Americans are both (as their newspapers assure us) "democratic," it gives a notion of how much the term covers! At any rate, in the older race there is a tradition of trained and cultivated politeness that flowers, at its best, into a simplicity democratic in the finest sense. Compared to it, our politeness is apt to be rather stagy, as our ease is at times a little boorish.

IV

It will be remembered that Paolo and
Francesca are met by Dante just beyond
the fatal gateway, in what might be called
the temperate zone of the infernal regions.
In the society of dangerously agreeable fel-
low-sinners they "go forever on the accursed
air," telling their beautiful tale to sympathis-
ing visitors from above; and as, unlike the
majority of mortal lovers, they seem not to
dread an eternity together, and as they feel
no exaggerated remorse for their sin, their
punishment is the mildest in the poet's list of
expiations.   There is all the width of hell
between the "Divine Comedy" and the "Scar-
let Letter"!

Far different is the lot of the dishonest man
of business and of the traitor to the state.   For
these two offenders against the political and
social order the ultimate horrors of the pit are
reserved.   The difference between their fate
and that of the lovers is like that between the

lot of an aviator in an eternally invulnerable
aeroplane and of a stoker in the burning hold
of an eternally torpedoed ship. On this distinction between the two classes of offences—
the antilegal and the antisocial—the whole
fabric of Latin morality is based.

The moralists and theologians of the Middle Ages, agitated as no other age has been
by the problem of death and the life after
death, worked out the great scheme of moral
retribution on which the "Divine Comedy"
is based. This system of punishment is the
result of a purely Latin and social conception of order. In it individualism has no
place. It is based on the interests of the family, and of that larger family formed by the
commune or the state; and it distinguishes,
implicitly if not outspokenly, between the
wrong that has far-reaching social conse-
quences and that which injures only one or
two persons, or perhaps only the moral sense
of the offender.

The French have continued to accept this

classification of offences. They continue to
think the sin against the public conscience far
graver than that against any private person.
If in France there is a distinction between
private and business morality it is exactly the
reverse of that prevailing in America, and
the French conscience rejects with abhor-
rence the business complaisances which the
rigidly virtuous American too often regards
as not immoral because not indictable. "Business" tends everywhere to subdue its victims
to what they work in, and it is not meant to
suggest that every French financier is irre-
proachable, or that France has not had more
than her share of glaring financial scandals,
but that among the real French, uncontam-
inated by cosmopolitan influences, and especially in the class of small shopkeepers and in
the upper bourgeoisie, business probity is
higher, and above all *more sensitive,* than in
America. It is not only, or always, through
indolence that France has remained backward in certain forms of efficiency.

It would be misleading to conclude that this sensitiveness is based on a respect for the rights of others. The French, it must be repeated, are as a race indifferent to the rights of others. In the people and the lower middle class (and how much higher up!) the traditional attitude is: "Why should I do my neighbour a good turn when he may be getting the better of me in some way I haven't found out?" The French are not generous, and they are not trustful. They do not willingly credit their neighbours with sentiments as disinterested as their own. But deep in their very bones is something that was called "the point of honour" when there was an aristocracy to lay exclusive claim to it, but that has, in reality, always permeated the whole fabric of the race. It is just as untranslatable as the "panache" into which it has flowered on so many immortal battle-fields; and it regulates the conscience of one of the most avaricious and least compassionate of peoples in their business relations, as it regulated the conduct in the field of the knights of chivalry and of the *parvenu* heroes of Napoleon.

It all comes back, perhaps, to the extraordinarily true French sense of values. As a people, the French have moral taste, and an ear for the "still small voice"; they know what is worth while, and they despise most of the benefits that accrue from a clever disregard of their own standards. It has been the fashion among certain of their own critics to inveigh against French "taste" and French "measure," and to celebrate the supposed lack of these qualities in the Anglo-Saxon races as giving a freer play to genius and a larger scope to all kinds of audacious enterprise. It is evident that if a new continent is to be made habitable, or a new prosody to be created, the business "point of honour" in the one case, and the French Academy in the other, may seriously hamper the task; but in the minor transactions of commerce and culture perhaps such restrictive influences are worth more to civilisation than a mediocre license.

v

Many years ago, during a voyage in the Mediterranean, the yacht on which I was cruising was driven by bad weather to take shelter in a small harbour on the Mainote coast. The country, at the time, was not considered particularly safe, and before landing we consulted the guide-book to see what reception we were likely to meet with.

This is the answer we found: "The inhabitants are brave, hospitable, and generous, but fierce, treacherous, vindictive, and given to acts of piracy, robbery, and wreckage."

Perhaps the foregoing attempt to define some attributes of the French character may seem as incoherent as this summary. At any rate, the endeavour to strike a balance between seemingly contradictory traits disposes one to indulgence toward the anonymous student of the Mainotes.

No civilised race has gone as unerringly as the French toward the natural sources of enjoyment; none has been so unashamed of instinct. Yet none has been more enslaved by social conventions, small complicated observances based on long-past conditions of life. No race has shown more collective magnanimity on great occasions, more pettiness and hardness in small dealings between individuals. Of no great people would it be truer to say that, like the Mainote tribesmen, they are generous and brave, yet fierce and vindictive. No people are more capable of improvising greatness, yet more afraid of the least initiative in ordinary matters. No people are more sceptical and more religious, more realistic and more romantic, more irritable and nervous, yet more capable of a long patience and a dauntless calm.

Such are the deductions which the foreign observer has made. It would probably take kinship of blood to resolve them into a harmonious interpretation of the French character.

All that the looker-on may venture is to say: Some of the characteristics I have noted seem unamiable, others dangerously disintegrating, others provokingly unprogressive. But when you have summed up the whole you will be forced to conclude that as long as enriching life is more than preserving it, as long as culture is superior to business efficiency, as long as poetry and imagination and reverence are higher and more precious elements of civilisation than telephones or plumbing, as long as truth is more bracing than hypocrisy, and wit more wholesome than dulness, so long will France remain greater than any nation that has not her ideals.

Once again it must be repeated that the best answer to every criticism of French weakness or French shortcomings is the conclusive one: *Look at the results!* Read her history, study her art, follow up the current of her ideas; then look about you, and you will see that the whole world is full of her spilt glory.

THE END (1)

About the Commentators

Diane de Margerie, born in Paris where she lives, is a renowned writer, novelist, and translator of Keats, Henry James, Edith Wharton, and Thomas Hardy. Not unlike Edith Wharton, she too spent her early years "abroad": a childhood in London and an adolescence in Peking. She stems from both a literary (grand-niece of Edmond Rostand) and a diplomatic background.

Mary Ann Caws, Distinguished Professor of English, French, and Comparative Literature at the Graduate School of the City University of New York, writes on art and literature (*The Eye in the Text*, *Women of Bloomsbury*, *The Surrealist Look*) and translates from the French, both modern poetry and prose.

ABOUT EDITH WHARTON RESTORATION
AND THE MOUNT

Edith Wharton Restoration, Inc., was founded in 1980 to preserve and restore Edith Wharton's home, The Mount, and to establish it as a cultural and educational center dedicated to the study and promotion of Edith Wharton, literature, and the design arts.

The Mount, located in Lenox, Massachusetts, is open to the public for tours and other programs from May through October each year. The house and gardens are currently undergoing an extensive long-term restoration. For information, contact: Edith Wharton Restoration, The Mount, P.O. Box 974, Lenox, MA 01240; telephone 413-637-1899, fax 413-637-0619.